C

SIR ARTHUR PINERO

SIR ARTHUR PINERO

A Critical Biography with Letters

By

WILBUR DWIGHT DUNKEL

KENNIKAT PRESS, INC./PORT WASHINGTON, N. Y.

TABLE OF CONTENTS

I

INTRODUCTORY

AN ORDINARY young man without much education becomes stage struck. He fails as an actor but writes plays.
His plays become amazingly popular. He wins wealth
and marries the young actress who played opposite him in one of
his first curtain-raisers. He takes himself and his work so seriously
that he tries to improve the technique of playwriting, discards
the old conventions of the soliloquy and the aside, and deals with
social problems when audiences wishing only to be amused refuse
to accept Ibsen's social plays. He writes independently and repu-
diates the suggestion that he imitates Ibsen, declaring that T. W.
Robertson, of the cup-and-saucer school, is his inspiration. He
cleverly adapts the French technique of the "well-made play" to
English social problems arising from the double standard of
morality and scores a hit.

Now he reaches the height of his attainment. He becomes a
member of the Garrick Club. King Edward VII recognizes his
achievement by bestowing a knighthood. His plays earn him
membership in the Royal Academy of Literature. Critics call him
the father of the modern English drama. But he continues to write
plays. His plays appear old fashioned. The revolts which he has
led now pass him by. His plays seem dated. He frantically strives
to resume his lost leadership. Younger critics forget his earlier
plays and smile at his present work. He retains his wealth. His
wife dies. And alone he bitterly reflects upon his sacrifice of
everything in order to write and re-write those plays now so
quickly forgotten. Such is the life of Pinero.

The purpose of this book is to explain how these incidents took
place. It is not my purpose to defend Pinero against his critics.
His plays must, as he himself said to me, stand for themselves.

1

But his career is no less interesting because of the present eclipse of his reputation. What he accomplished will remain of interest, as it already has, in any history of the modern English drama.

His life presents an excellent point of view from which to consider the development of the formula for writing plays, now widely used in the contemporary theater. For the reader who would understand how plays developed into the present form, study of Pinero's career holds particular interest.

When I first entered Pinero's study he asked, "Why do you want to write a book about me, about my plays?"

"Because you wrote *The Second Mrs. Tanqueray*, and I can find out so little about you!"

He asked me if I had read Hamilton Fyfe's two books and at my nod of assent continued, "You have an opportunity to correct many errors of fact."

And so I began to read through the newspaper and magazine files in the Colindale Branch of the British Museum, searching for the first-night evaluations of not only Pinero's plays but those of his contemporaries. From his first London hit in 1880 through 1909 the reviewers praised the majority of his plays, almost without one dissenting voice. But Shaw began the attack which was to become a roar of disapproval after 1909. Those early critics had standards, however. Such men as A. B. Walkley of the *London Times*, Clement Scott of the *Daily Telegraph*, who completely misunderstood Ibsen's work, and William Archer, who translated Ibsen's plays and lectured about him with rare understanding for those days, all agreed on Pinero's contribution.

I agree, furthermore, with the later critics that Pinero failed utterly to live in the new social order brought on by the World War. With the new society he was completely out of tune. Had he retired in 1910, his reputation would doubtless have suffered less decline.

The chief difficulty in evaluating Pinero's work lies in the fact that his play must be judged in the theater, not from the printed page. His dialogue becomes for the reader artificial, even turgid. Pinero was really not a literary playwright. His plays must be seen if the wizardry of his stagecraft is to be appreciated. And Tallulah Bankhead's revival of *The Second Mrs. Tanqueray* in the summer theaters during 1940 supports this contention. For this play, forty-eight years old, surprised one critic after another; its bones did not creak; the master-craftsman's work had passed its test.

It is not too much to hope that other plays from his pen may be tried and found satisfying in the present-day theater, but their subject matter, the problems arising from the double standard of morality, must for this generation at least remain hopelessly dated.

Despite these conditions the record of Pinero's achievement merits careful study because of his place in the development of the modern English drama. And even though his life was lacking in colorful experiences, his story is the ageless theme of tragedy.

It is ironical that Pinero, who wrote discerningly about the lack of theatrical talent in Robert Browning and Robert Louis Stevenson, should have lacked their dramatic genius. Both Browning and Stevenson failed to write plays suitable for production in the theater, although they presented memorable conflicts between significant personalities. Both Browning and Stevenson, furthermore, surpassed Pinero as skilful users of language, finding the right words and felicitous phrases. Their plays consequently are readable.

There would be less point to writing this book if Pinero had not struggled to be a literary man as well as a playwright. Though he did not write poetry and novels, he did raise the standard of the literary quality of the drama as he found it. But the standard was very low when he began writing plays in the seventies. Men of literary genius were not then writing for the theater. Its requirements antagonized superior novelists and poets in England. The demand was primarily for plays which would exhibit the talents of the powerful actor-managers. This type of play Pinero could write, for he himself had been an actor and knew what the actor-managers wanted.

Pinero was not content to be a purveyor of plays to the

actor-managers. He wanted recognition as an author. The rising fame of Ibsen in the free theaters on the Continent and among the university audiences in England doubtless irked him, though Ibsen offered no competition to Pinero in the commercial theaters in London. Pinero always denied Ibsen's influence. So did Henry Arthur Jones, who for twenty-five years was Pinero's chief competitor in the London theaters. But probably they both wished to claim for England the new advance in playwriting.

Pinero's talent was stagecraft. He knew how to organize material for effective presentation on the stage. He understood the mass psychology, the emotional reaction of the group in the theater, and thought little of the individual reader. As a result the dialogue in his plays is right for the actor and disconcerting to the reader. Phrases which annoy the cultivated reader ring true on the stage. But in particular Pinero was the master of suspense, motivating the turns in his plot sequence with unerring skill. For he understood stage business, the timing of motion and sound, and, above all, the reactions of an audience to the physical properties on the stage itself.

Unlike Henry Arthur Jones, Pinero wrote few articles and no books about the theater and dramatic technique. Unlike Oscar Wilde, Pinero avoided the fashionable drawing-rooms. Unlike Shaw, Pinero refused to talk about himself.

While Shaw and Ibsen were startling the world with their iconoclastic ideas, Pinero shocked London playgoers with his forthright treatment of the double standard of morality, a subject strictly unmentionable then. But Pinero's handling of the theme was so effective that his revolt won acceptance; then he was left without a subject. He seemed unable to grasp the implications in the social changes taking place in the twentieth century. His devotion to the theater and the meager glimpse of life he had gained in his early days in a law office failed him in the end. He saw life only in terms of the stage.

His innovations in dramatic technique were widely copied and soon became the stock in trade of every aspiring young playwright. But his younger contemporaries possessed greater intellectual capacity; they could write about ideas and appeal to readers as well as to playgoers. Their plays of reform and social protest made Pinero's plays appear more artificial than possibly they actually were in stagecraft, though hopelessly dated in substance.

Pinero's failures thus become interesting not only because of the height of his success but in relation to the development of the drama which took place during his lifetime.

II

STAGE-STRUCK BOY

IN THE affairs of men the accidents of when and where birth, childhood, and education take place may not matter very much. In the case of Pinero these conditions determine his life; in fact, an understanding of these conditions explains many of the problems in his biography; they form not only his personality but the character of his work.

Arthur Wing Pinero was born on May 24, 1855. This was, as the record will show, precisely the right time to be born for a spectacular career in the theater as a playwright, for new and original plays were not at this time being written for the English theater. There were of course lavish productions of Shakespeare's plays, with the emphasis upon eloquent rendition of famous lines and the ensemble discarded. Some Restoration and eighteenth-century comedies and a few closet dramas, written by poets and novelists for the reading public, were produced. But the popular entertainments in the theaters, in addition to the shows in the music halls, were chiefly French farces and German melodramas, stolen by shorthand writers for a pittance and produced without payment of royalty fees.

In such a market there was no opportunity to make a living by writing original plays. But in the history of English literature, a history of convention and revolt, an extreme condition has always been followed by a reaction to it. This was certain to take place in the matter of writing plays. And new leaders in writing plays were just as certain to emerge. Henry Arthur Jones, George Bernard Shaw, James Barrie, and Pinero were all born within this period of a few years, from 1854 to 1860. Others too came along at just this time, but they had either less to say or less skill in saying it than their more famous contemporaries.

Pinero was born at 21 Dalby Terrace, Islington, in the north-eastern section of London. Today Islington is a drab district, known for its markets, warehouses, and manufacturing plants. Then, as Pinero himself recalled it, "it was a pleasant enough locality."

Near his home was a famous theater, Sadler's Wells. Now on the site of the old playhouse stands a new and rather unattractive building, bearing the same name, competently operated under the same management as the now more famous "Old Vic," across the Thames River, near Waterloo Station.

The influence of Sadler's Wells remained with Pinero throughout his life. His popular comedy, *Trelawny of the "Wells,"* in which John Drew and a distinguished cast appeared on tour across America, revealed Pinero's sentimental attachment to the old Sadler's Wells. For there his dreams began. His first sweethearts were the actresses to whom the small boy perched on a bench in the pit could not express his affection. But he never forgot them; his love remained pure and constant!

His family was well to do when he was born. The Pinheiros had migrated to England early in the eighteenth century. They were originally Portuguese Jews. Mark Pinero, the playwright's grandfather, changed the original spelling of the family name to Pinero. He married well, a relative of Thomas Wing, who fought at the Victory of Trafalgar. Mark Pinero became a successful solicitor and established the family in cosmopolitan London.

Mark Pinero's son, John Daniel Pinero, followed his father in the law. He married Lucy Daines. She too came from an old English family. They had two daughters, Mrs. Francis Paine and Miss Mary Pinero, both living at Arthur's death. When Arthur was born, however, his father was well past middle age; never able, to the playwright's recollection, to take much interest in his young son.

John and Lucy Pinero were liberal-minded parents. They enjoyed the theater and took their children with them. "Pin" recalled that when he was a mere infant his parents took him to see a pantomime at the Grecian Theatre in the City Road. And while they had money, they were quite willing to give him the necessary eighteen pence for a seat in the pit at Sadler's Wells. It was there, consequently, as a small boy that he spent much of his time, quite hopelessly stage struck.

Pinero's parents, however, had no other thought for his future than his following his father and his grandfather in the law; nevertheless, they were tolerant of his interest in the theater. In contrast may be cited the experience of Henry Arthur Jones, Pinero's first great rival in writing plays. Jones's parents were nonconformists, in their way sincerely religious folk, who would not permit their son to attend a theatrical production. In fact Jones was eighteen when he first saw a professional production in the theater. Such experience likewise came late to that talented Scottish lad, James Barrie, whose family sacrificed everything for his education in a good school and in the University of Edinburgh. But Shaw, born in Dublin, was not restricted by his parents; there was simply no theater for him to attend until, at twenty-one, he followed his mother and sister to London. Pinero consequently had the advantage of familiarity with the theater from his childhood.

The significance of childhood experiences may readily be overstated. All of these playwrights learned how to arrange material so as to be effective on the stage; nevertheless, Pinero became the perfect craftsman of them all; that must be admitted, however far he may have fallen behind the attainment of Shaw or Barrie in thought and expression.

While Arthur was still a small boy in school he felt the pinch of poverty. His father's once flourishing practice gradually diminished to the point where there was to be derived scarcely any income whatsoever. At this juncture Arthur was withdrawn from school and sent to work in his father's office.

His father had had offices in South Square, in famous old Gray's Inn, and in Prince Street, since renamed Bedford Row. His office was now in Great James Street. So from the school in Exmouth Street, Clerkenwell, Arthur moved to his father's office. He was only ten. But he had to become his father's "right hand."

This youngster with the large head, bold features, and stocky body became a very serious-minded young man. He found the law dull and loathed it. From time to time he gained some private tutoring. But his mind was centered on the theater.

And just at this time took place an event which was important not only for this youngster of ten but for the future of the English drama. Marie Wilton, a popular young actress, leased the Prince of Wales's Theatre in Tottenham Street. It was a small bandbox theater located outside the fashionable district. But she had ideas. She carpeted the floor of the auditorium and commenced to look around for plays suitable for her small stage.

Marie Wilton's discovery of Tom Robertson and the subsequent beginning of the cup-and-saucer drama cannot be overestimated. For Tom Robertson's plays had been rejected by every other manager in London. Nothing happened in them. The characters just sat and talked. This lack of action appealed to Miss Wilton, mindful as she was of the limited space on her stage. So she produced Tom Robertson's *Society*. She assembled for this production an excellent cast, including Squire Bancroft. The play as well as the direction were both different from anything heretofore presented in London. In fact this type of work actually was independent of what Ibsen was attempting at the National Theatre in Christiania.

Some days passed before the carriage trade heard of the production. In time, going to Miss Wilton's intimate playhouse became the thing for London society to do. As *Society* became a glorious success, she made money and accepted more rejected manuscripts from the befriended playwright. And so the old "utility-actor," Tom Robertson, found production for his queer plays, which were to set the fashion for many years to come.

Miss Wilton instituted many innovations in production which Sir Henry Irving was later to use with even greater success. She insisted upon realism: that the stage should represent a drawing-room with the fourth wall removed. No actor spoke to the audience. The dialogue actually became conversation. Actors even talked in low tones, with their backs to the audience, just as if the audience had not paid to be entertained. In furnishings for the stage the style of the day was used, however inharmonious with the play; the costumes were incongruous, for no actress was accustomed to appear on the stage in anything except an evening gown. Marie Wilton changed all this. Verisimilitude on the English stage begins with her productions. But the credit is usually given either to Ibsen or to Sir Henry Irving.

These productions were an inspiration to Arthur Pinero, and he never missed an opportunity to pay his tribute to Tom Robertson and the Bancrofts for what they taught him; for Marie Wilton had fallen in love with Squire Bancroft and married him. A few years later, at the height of their careers, they retired, to live as Sir Squire and Lady Bancroft of Berkeley Square.

But to return to Pinero. He was now fifteen, and his father's health made retirement imperative. This change came in 1870. It was something of a relief for Arthur, though it meant seeking employment elsewhere, for his father's carelessness about minor matters had got on the boy's nerves. In fact the concern for small, seemingly unimportant details, which characterized Arthur's attitude throughout life, may well have become established in his personality during these impressionable years. This mania for precision, which disturbed everyone who tried to work with Pinero, became not only his greatest personal fault but the secret of his success as a writer and director in the theater.

A single illustration suffices to show the importance of Arthur's reaction to his father's carelessness. Solicitors were required to register each year, but in 1865, when Arthur joined his father in the office, the boy was puzzled to discover that his father's name did not appear in annual, legal registry; upon his insistence his father did qualify, though the year was well advanced. But each year the youngster had to argue with his father in vain to register on time; nevertheless, this irregular procedure continued until 1870, when the elder Pinero retired and moved to his country place near Greenwich.

Arthur's first independent job was a clerkship in the Circulating Library, Ltd., located on Wigmore Street. After a few months of this he resumed his study of the law, going to work for a solicitor with offices in Lincoln's Inn Fields. But this position did not appeal to him, as it did to the majority of other youngsters thus employed, as an apprenticeship to a career. He performed the routine duties without imagination. His thoughts were about the theater, in particular concerned with the innovations at the Prince of Wales's Theatre.

During these years he regularly attended the night classes at Birkbeck Institute. The subject of chief interest to him was elocution. And he finally graduated, giving the role of Hamlet as the climax of his work. Meanwhile, however, he devoted his noon hours daily to standing opposite the Garrick Club, watching important barristers and authors enter and leave its impressive portals.

Years later, at a testimonial dinner given in his honor by the members of the Garrick Club, Pinero described these experiences of his stage-struck youth. When he was earning from his employment in Lincoln's Inn Fields approximately five dollars a week, much of this small sum went into the common purse at home. His meager lunch required little time for its consumption. So, rain or shine, he would hurry away to watch the important-appearing persons entering and leaving the Garrick Club. But of course as the youngster observed its members day after day, he frequently mistook an eminent barrister for a popular comedian. The Garrick Club thus became the goal of his life, and he never lost interest in it during the forty-odd years of his membership.

In the evenings he went to the theater whenever he could. This constant and unfailing interest, this concentration upon a single way of life, this absorption of everything theatrical available to him, certainly explains why he later had only one increasing purpose—the writing of plays. As a boy he had no interest in any of the usual activities of boyhood. During these teen years he matured rapidly; he had the attitude of a serious man, throwing all his strength into this one channel of activity. This was as much a fault as a source of power, for the playwright must see life whole; he must know society in the drawing-room as well as on the stage; he must understand the lighthearted as well as the serious-minded; he must understand the other man's point of view if he would explain the meaning of life in universal terms.

The chief criticism to be brought against Pinero's plays is their theatricality, their lack of breadth and vision beyond the stage. But granted this weakness, his work has the compensating strength of being nearly perfect on the stage. And his strength has been underestimated by those critics obsessed with his weakness. Hence it has not been easy to form a fair and accurate estimate of Pinero's contribution, but that is the reason for this book.

III

APPRENTICESHIP

YOUNG Arthur Pinero was not merely stage struck; he was determined to do something in the theater. He knew enough about acting not only from seeing plays but from studying elocution at the Birkbeck Institute to realize that he was not prepared to qualify as an actor. But about writing he knew nothing at all! So he decided to startle the London actor-managers with plays of his own writing.

He soon discovered, however, that here he also had a real handicap. Through lack of normal attendance at school and familiarity only with wordy prose of legal documents, he was ill prepared to develop a style which would excite professional play-readers to wonder. As a matter of fact, he only aroused their profanity.

But he was persistent to a fault. After failing to win the attention of the actor-managers with his posted manuscripts, he called upon them personally. But this method brought no results. Finally, he hit upon the use of his employer's stationery, seeking by means of this association with the eminent and the Lincoln's Inn Fields's address to win attention. In his old age—when I came to know him—he delighted in recalling one incident in particular.

One of the high and mighty actor-managers replied to Pinero's employer. Inadvertently that worthy solicitor read the letter intended for his young law clerk.

DEAR SIR:

Your stuff is of no earthly use to me. For God's sake, fetch it away as soon as possible.

And so ended in embarrassment and utter frustration Pinero's first attempts at becoming a dramatic author. But it served at least this purpose: he had clarified his mind on one point, namely, the kind of people about whom he wished to write. They were characters of wealth and leisure. Even though he did not know the language they spoke, except as he picked up phrases and sentences around the office, his interest in such people became fixed, never to be changed throughout his long career.

In retrospect, Pinero defended this attitude of his by saying that those people had sufficient money to do interesting things, such as getting into trouble with the law. For Pinero saw society always in terms of a solicitor's office. The contracts there drawn up involved lust, greed, and revenge! And these moral weaknesses of humanity became the themes of his cynically tempered plays.

When he was nineteen his father died, and the family's affairs were set in order. His mother no longer required his support, though he had little to offer. For the peak of his pecuniary attainment in the profession of his father and grandfather, after two raises in his weekly salary, had reached one pound ten, or approximately seven and one-half dollars. So, upon his father's death, he decided to give up the law, without completing his articles, and follow a career in the theater.

Just at this time Londoners were hearing about Mr. and Mrs. R. H. Wyndham and the stock company they were leading at the Theatre Royal in Edinburgh. Their experiments in productions were reputedly brilliant, and they were establishing themselves to such an extent that everyone informed about theatrical affairs knew that it was only a matter of time before the Wyndhams would come to London.

Therefore young Arthur set out for Edinburgh and fortunately got a place for himself in their company as a "general utility." In English stock companies of the day, this position was not much to write home about. His remuneration was the usual pound a week, a third less, to be sure, than he had earned in Lincoln's Inn Fields, but he was happy now.

In Edinburgh, Pinero found happiness for the first time in his life—the pleasure which comes with congenial work and the feeling of accomplishment. In the last year of his life he recalled his

experiences of those days much as an American might sentimentalize about his first employer or Alma Mater. The years had
either dimmed the memory of unpleasant incidents or placed them
in true perspective.

Pinero's new work actually meant little to his development.
The company presented a new play each week, thus permitting
slight opportunity for an inexperienced actor to learn more than
his own small part and catch a glimpse of what the leading members of the company were doing. For the value of training in a
stock company, and it is very important indeed, lies in the necessity of memorizing new parts and defining new personalities week
in and week out; in a word, the benefit was beyond Pinero's in-
experience. But he did learn how to walk.

Sometimes he appeared in two or three parts within a single
production, merely changing his costume to conform to the different character listed on the program. He rarely had a word to
say. He recalled appearing as the Swell with Dundreary whiskers. These the Clown shaved off with a wooden razor. But
those experiences had their compensations. He had time to read
plays in which he took part and to study their construction as
well as the Wyndhams' expert direction.

His living conditions formed his chief problem. When he arrived in Edinburgh he had registered at a well-known hotel, but
he soon discovered that he could not afford it on his small salary.
Then he moved to what the Scots still call a temperance hotel,
and there he had an amusing experience.

One day an elderly gentleman, who did not look at all like a
devotee of temperance, confided in Pinero a curious quirk in the
law of Scotland. If one went early to bed in a temperance hotel
and then rang the bell violently and complained of illness, the
landlord was obliged under heavy penalty of the law to bring a
bottle of whiskey to the ailing guest and leave it at the bedside.
Pinero, however, could not afford even this temperance hotel.
So he moved to a theatrical boarding-house of the kind where the
landlady was casually addressed as "Ma."

One morning, after he had been in Edinburgh for not quite a year, he was returning from a walk and saw a huge fire. The Theatre Royal was in flames. It burned to the ground. And he was without a job, for the Wyndhams had to break up their company, since there was no other place for their work and the rebuilding would take a very long time.

Pinero moved to Liverpool, with good recommendations from the Wyndhams. Again he was lucky and got a part as a "walking gentleman" in a play written by the well-known novelist, Wilkie Collins. The part was unimportant. What counted was that the popular Mr. Collins had written the play and consequently came to see its production. And he saw Pinero and liked him immediately! This of course was sheer luck, but the ability to meet people and win their friendship was becoming for Pinero a highly developed talent.

Just at this time Collins was excited about the dramatization of his popular novel, *Armadale*, and thought Pinero was the type to play the character of Mr. Darch in the forthcoming production of the play in London.

Collins wrote about Pinero to R. C. Carton, who was dramatizing the novel. Carton was not only a popular playwright of the day but the influential actor-manager of the Globe Theatre in London. Pinero, thus introduced to Carton, agreed to terms and returned home at twenty-one, a full-fledged actor.

The outstanding actor-manager in London at this time was Sir Henry Irving. Ably supported by the beautiful and vivacious Ellen Terry, he was producing Shakespearean plays at the Lyceum Theatre. His company enjoyed the distinction reflected from his brilliant acting, and he was rapidly becoming the dictator of theatrical destinies. Though the Bancrofts were still playing at the little Prince of Wales's Theatre with undiminished popularity, their influence was considerably less than Irving's.

One afternoon Irving dropped into the Globe Theatre to see Carton's production and discovered Pinero. He was so much impressed with Pinero's work that after the performance he took the trouble to call upon the young actor. Pinero was overwhelmed.

When *Armadale* closed, Irving immediately invited Pinero to join the company at the Lyceum. Pinero gladly accepted this opportunity to become associated with the most popular company in London.

Squire Bancroft then came to Pinero and asked him to assist with some research at the British Museum for information concerning the life at Bath in the eighteenth century. This material Bancroft felt he must have for the production of Sheridan's *The Rivals*. Pinero again was overjoyed to work with Bancroft, the idol of his boyhood. And subsequently Pinero appeared as Sir Anthony Absolute in the Bancrofts' production.

Meanwhile, Pinero continued as a member of Irving's company, appearing in minor roles. But he was rapidly gaining a reputation as a character actor, particularly successful in the roles of old men. He was careful in the study of his part and expert enough, but he seemed to lack the ability which would eventually bring him to stardom, as the theater was then organized. He played such roles as King Claudius and Guildenstern in *Hamlet* and Salerno in *The Merchant of Venice* with Sir Henry Irving in London and then toured the United Kingdom with him. Irving realized that this young man of twenty-two could be relied upon to conduct himself like a veteran; nevertheless, the record is rather clear that Pinero had before him no remarkable career as an actor.

Too much has been made, however, of the opinion of the Manchester critic who declared that Pinero's playing of King Claudius was the poorest he had ever seen! Pinero's style was probably too advanced for the provincial critic. For, as Pinero gained in confidence, he was to go far beyond the experiments of the Bancrofts and Irving; he was later to demand of the companies which he rehearsed in his own plays absolute realism of the degree not even surpassed in American theaters by the late David Belasco.

Whatever Pinero lacked as an actor, the record is clear that in rapid succession, within a scant two years, he had won the esteem of Mr. and Mrs. Wyndham, Wilkie Collins, R. C. Carton, Henry

Irving and Ellen Terry, and Squire and Marie Bancroft, the leading actor-managers of the day. If that is failure, certainly many young actors now forgotten would have exchanged places with him; for these distinguished people of the theater always spoke and wrote of him in the highest regard, as indicated in their memoirs, letters, and interviews. And this attitude toward Pinero was to continue. He won the confidence of all his distinguished contemporaries except George Bernard Shaw.

Everyone emphasized his seriousness, studious attitude, and meticulous attention to details. He may not have been a brilliant performer, but he knew how the job should be done. In short, he was a director before that theatrical personage existed.

During his twenty-second year he had his first play produced. It was just a one-act play, designed to be a "curtain-lifter." For in those days in the London theater it was customary to give a brief play before the play of the evening. This was not a bad custom. Not only were the late diners thus accommodated, but young authors had a chance to display their talent without the risk involved in producing a complete play. Pinero's piece was entitled *£200 a Year*.

This was produced in October, 1877, at the Globe Theatre. Though Pinero was a member of Irving's company, R. C. Carton had not forgotten the young actor he had introduced to London playgoers. Carton thus became the one to start Pinero on the long road he was to follow as a playwright. The performance was a benefit for F. H. Macklin and thus gained an important audience. Pinero himself appeared in the cast, which included Miss Compton, the wife of Mr. Carton. The short play was well received; its author was regarded as a young writer of promise. Pinero had found himself; and he set to work at once to do another play.

But the enormous royalties which he was to receive in years to come never meant quite as much as the set of links and studs given him by Mr. Carton for this first play.

Irving was in the audience and became much interested in his young actor's ambition to write plays. As a result, he was ready to produce Pinero's next play, *Two Can Play at That Game*, and paid five pounds for it. Like the first, it was only a "curtain-lifter." But Pinero had done a much better job of writing.

More than a year passed before Pinero again approached Irving with a playscript, but he was so eager to have it produced that he offered it to Irving without royalties. Irving produced it at the Lyceum Theatre on September 20, 1879. And *Daisy's Escape* was such a success that Irving gave Pinero fifty pounds for it. This was generous remuneration for a "curtain-lifter" at that time, an indication certainly of the progress Pinero was making in learning how to write.

Of almost equal importance to the success of this play was, however, a discovery Pinero made on this occasion: He found himself in love. It came about this way. He had again acted in his own play, but opposite him this time was the talented and lovely young actress, Myra Holme. She interpreted her part so sympathetically that he knew he owed much of the success of his play to her. She was extraordinarily beautiful. And Pinero was so excited about her that he simply fell in love.

Myra Holme was the widow of Captain Angus L. Hamilton. And from this tragic marriage she had a small daughter, also named Myra. To the daughter Pinero began writing letters filled with humor and sentiment to amuse the child. These letters are still preserved by Mrs. Claude Neville Hughes of London, the Myra to whom they were addressed.

But though the child responded to young Pinero's attentions, the mother was determined to win a higher place for herself in the theater. Her ambition did not permit a second marriage, particularly since Pinero wanted her to leave the stage. And Pinero himself was neither an established playwright nor a popular actor. At this point his future was far from determined.

He was writing steadily, but so slowly, with so much revision required, that his accomplishment seemed slight. *Bygones*, another one-act comedy, was presented at the Lyceum Theatre on September 18, 1880, but he had finished it in December of the preceding year. However, *Hester's Mystery*, finished in May of

1880, was produced at the Folly Theatre on June 5, 1880. But he had yet to score a hit with a long play which would bring him sufficient money to settle down to the task of becoming a professional writer.

Irving urged Pinero to abandon acting and devote all of his time to playwriting. That was just want he wanted to do, but he also knew what the pinch of poverty meant. There was security in Irving's company, and he stayed with Irving for five years, though he gradually took more time for his writing.

To become a commercial playwright in the 1880's was not to follow a blueprint. The new plays Pinero realized were chaotic in technique. The authors were not keeping up with the rapid advance in method of staging. So he decided to do something about it, strike out along the plot manipulation developed by the French authors, Scribe and Sardou, and suffuse the action with English attitude toward moral problems. For Pinero was methodical to a fault; he had to know precisely what he wanted to do; he was not a maker of scintillating phrases; his was not a brilliant, impulsive wit.

Above all else in the formation of Pinero's early technique was the thought of how an incident would be handled on the stage. He was primarily concerned with theatrical effectiveness. He was certainly not a literary man adapting his material to the requirements of the stage. Consequently, Pinero's plays in the hands of unimaginative and untheatrically minded readers become lifeless, rather stiff, quite stilted in style. But the actors and actresses know that for the stage these literary faults do not exist. Here, then, is the perfect example of the difference between literary excellence and theatrically practicable style.

Browning, one of the most dramatic of all the English poets, wrote in a style unsuited for stage use. The actors could not mouth the long sentences which appeal to the reader as the essence of dramatic verve. But after an author's plays are no longer presented on the stage, the reader is both judge and jury.

This is not to say that Pinero profited by his tremendous lack of literary background. But it is necessary to judge a man's work on the basis of what he attempted to do and how well he succeeded in that particular attempt. The critical procedure in the case of Pinero's work has been to point out his obvious lack of literary finesse and then fail to realize that his plays for this reason were suited to the requirements of actors and actresses on the stage. And the record of his career from 1880 until the first World War cannot honestly be denied by any fair-minded person.

In his time in the London theaters there was no literary tradition to follow; the successful playwrights were actors. Most of them were imitators either of Robertson's cup-and-saucer comedies or of the French well-made play, *pièce bien faite*. But neither was profound. The aim of Robertson and his followers was to amuse with conversation by creating the impression that the audience was eavesdropping. Both Scribe and Sardou sought to interest the audience in action by skilful manipulation of incidents, producing surprise and suspense.

The reason for this peculiar state of theatrical affairs was the direct result of the continuation of the old royal patents, established in 1660, until 1843. Though for a hundred years there was no reason to prohibit the production of English plays in all the theaters except the royalty theaters, this was the condition. Both Drury Lane and Covent Gardens had original patents; and the Haymarket had annually been given the same license. All the other theaters were nominally music halls until 1843, though they were not restricted to variety programs; they could produce foreign plays, and they did so with great success.

By act of Parliament in 1843 the theaters were liberated, permitting production of English plays in any theater which sought a license for such productions. As a result, conditions were immediately chaotic. Every actor-manager sought to produce Shakespeare's plays and those of other traditional writers, if only for his own reputation. But the long-maintained restrictions had forced authors to be literary—writers of essays, novels, and poetry. So into the new field of playwriting rushed actors, determined to keep the theater for themselves.

Coleridge had written poetical plays after the manner of Schiller, who in turn owed his inspiration and technique to Shake-speare. Shelley and Byron made half-hearted attempts to write for the theater, but both were content to have their verse dramas read by readers. Tennyson's plays too were closet dramas. But Browning, encouraged by William Macready, tried again and again to win a public in the theater. Browning's fault, as Arthur Pinero has pointed out, was not his lack of dramatic quality but his ignorance of what was practicable on the stage. Alone of all the literary men in the nineteenth century, Bulwer-Lytton achieved success, particularly with *Richelieu*, *The Lady of Lyons*, and *Money*.

Owing to these conditions any criticism of Pinero's apprentice-ship must emphasize his associates in the theater. Pinero himself held Sir Henry Irving's opinions in highest regard.

Irving was a strict disciplinarian; he ruled his company on the stage and in private life. Like the Bancrofts, Irving desired to elevate the social position of actors and actresses, which, in a class-conscious country, was at the time very low indeed. His manner may doubtless have seemed to many as pompous, but he honestly regarded the theater as a high calling and did as much as any man to combat its low moral and social reputation.

Pinero was consequently much incensed when in his late years he was described as having perpetrated a joke on Irving. It was a harmless jest, concerning Irving's desire to have the company on stage to watch his direction of minor details, and in this instance the posting of a notice for everyone in the company to watch the carpenter fix a piece of scenery.

Some actor sick and tired of watching Irving rehearse a seem-ingly unimportant bit of stage business might have posted that notice, but certainly not Pinero, for he lacked a sense of humor about the theater; in fact, his attitude was precisely like Irving's.

Meanwhile, Henry Arthur Jones, a young commercial traveler, was writing melodramas while riding on trains or in hotel rooms after his orders and reports were finished for the day. He had slight formal education and no interest in acting, but he was learning how to create exciting incidents. His chief problem was his large family, which kept him busy earning a regular income instead of taking time off to write a play.

James Barrie at this time had finished his excellent education at Edinburgh and was now writing short stories and novels, which the London editors could not understand. But despite the handicap in such a market he was overcoming his Scottish dialect and rapidly winning a reading public.

George Bernard Shaw was a clerk in a Dublin land office, comfortably earning a decent salary in a position of security. But he was eager to follow his mother and sister to London. And when he did so in the next few months, he began a period of frenzied writing which lasted for nine years, and he earned from his total output less than the equivalent of ten dollars.

The turning-point in Pinero's apprenticeship came in 1880, when he finished *The Money Spinner*. This full-length play about gamblers, cards, and horses was given a trial production at the Theatre Royal in Manchester on November 5, 1880. The characters all had unclean hands; not a single person was admirable; even the heroine cheated. Critics and audiences were puzzled, but they liked the play.

Meanwhile, in London, Mr. and Mrs. Kendall in association with John Hare, all old friends of Pinero, were managing the St. James's Theatre. They agreed to produce the play and presented it to London playgoers on January 8, 1881, as a two-act play; the first act entitled *The Ferret* was omitted. It became Pinero's first hit. The critics recognized a new quality and praised it. That new quality was Pinero's refusal to compromise. He did not sentimentalize about wrongdoing, nor did he become a reformer. He offered a cynical comedy unlike anything since the work of Congreve and Wycherley in the last quarter of the seventeenth century.

The next August he repeated this success with his new play, *Imprudence*. Everyone in the boarding-house, the scene of this play, was selfish, narrow minded, and mean. The same cynical spirit suffused the action.

In the autumn of this same year, 1881, was produced his third long play, *The Squire*. But this play was a tragedy, quite different from the two bitter farce comedies which had preceded it; nevertheless, it added to the reputation of the young playwright, though it did not surpass *The Money Spinner* in popularity.

Pinero had taken the London theaters by storm with these three plays. Everyone began to talk about him and his work, but he refused to be stampeded by society; he refused interviews; he continued to write plays in the same slow, painstaking way. As a result, many people were disappointed and critical.

In 1882 Jones scored his first London hit with *The Silver King*. This melodrama became more popular than any of Pinero's unpleasant plays. Its characters were done in bold strokes; they were either absolutely pure or completely bad. Evildoers paid for their sins. Of course Pinero's characters were different from Jones's, much more like human beings, mixtures of good intentions and bad deeds, without being punished.

Pinero's development during the next two years was insignificant, though he continued to appeal at the box offices. It was simply commercial success. But such a statement, common enough in critical surveys of the drama, seems, nevertheless, not only smug but unfair. In our present-day theater men strive for commercial success and receive high praise for achieving it; in fact, the unproduced playwright, however artistic his work may be, receives no praise until he obtains production for his work. And to have his work produced, he must offer his play to the commercial theater.

In other words, hypocrisy abounds in the criticism of the drama. For if the play is successful, it is damned as merely commercial. If it fails, few defenders of it come forth to support the young playwright's next adventure, for everyone remembers the failure. A young writer may then be well advised to write for financial independence, as did both Pinero and Jones, and hope that afterward he can present art for art's sake and reveal his beautiful soul.

The difficulty with this advice is that too often the playwright forms habits of technique which he cannot shake off when he wishes to become an artist. He has learned to depend upon clichés, old tried-and-true devices, and the quick appeal as opposed to the valid. Jones discovered this. Even his mature social plays retained the melodramatic quality of his first commercial successes.

Pinero was striving for money in these years and getting it. *Girls and Boys*, originally entitled *Human Nature: A Village Love Story*, was produced at Toole's Theatre on November 1, 1882. *The Rector* was produced on March 24, 1883, at the Court Theatre; *Lords and Commons* was produced at the Haymarket Theatre on November 24, 1883. The production at the Haymarket was the last by Sir Squire and Lady Bancroft before their retirement from the stage; otherwise, the three plays have no significance.

But Pinero had made money. Four years had passed since Myra Holme had acted in the curtain lifter with him, and he had wooed her with the same persistence that characterized his determination to become a playwright. So they married and moved to 64 St. John's Wood Road. But she had refused to retire from her career on the stage, despite Pinero's insistence on her doing so.

How far Pinero had advanced in the world of the theater may be readily grasped from the implications in the following letter. Letters from contemporaries give the immediate point of view, so often lost to the biographer.

> 90, GLOUCESTER PLACE
> PORTMAN SQUARE, W.
> 28th May 1883

DEAR MR. PINERO,

I have myself suffered so much from illness that I can sincerely sympathise with Mrs. Pinero. If I can only feel as sure of her ability to encounter the fatigue of rehearsing as I feel of the interest which she is good enough to take in her part—I shall be perfectly satisfied.

I well remember the funny actor who interested us in those past days—and I heartily congratulate him on the position to which he has risen as a dramatic author.

The first half of the play is beginning to "look alive." I hope to rehearse the second half tomorrow.

Believe me, Dear Mr. Pinero

> Faithfully yours,
> WILKIE COLLINS

This letter also suggests an important feature of style in its formalism. The late Victorians were stilted in their social relationships, as everyone knows. But the present generation of critics seems to forget this point in judging late Victorian plays and demands the colloquial idiom of our time. The absence of colloquial phrases in Pinero's formal dialogue was proper and realistic. In fact, when he later tried to use the free style of the twentieth century, his dialogue became turgid.

This is certainly not an attempt to admire Pinero's stilted dialogue but rather an explanation so obvious that someone might have observed long ago that the Victorians were Victorians! This is true of morals as well as speech.

The Rocket, another potboiler, was tried out at the Prince of Wales's Theatre in Liverpool and then produced at the Gaiety Theatre in London on December 10, 1883. One month later *Low-Water* was produced at the Globe Theatre, on January 12, 1884. In May, *The Iron Master*, an adaptation of Georges Ohnet's *Le Maître de forges* was produced at the St. James's Theatre. In September, *In Chancery* was tried out at the Lyceum Theatre in Edinburgh and produced at the Gaiety Theatre in London on December 24, 1884.

Four long plays within a year! And the adaptation from the French cannot be dismissed as merely a translation, as the following letter from Pinero to Clement Scott, the dramatic critic of the *Daily Telegraph*, explains:

> 10 MARLBOROUGH CRESCENT
> BEDFORD PARK, CHISWICK
> 30th Oct. 1884

MY DEAR SCOTT,

I had written a note to you when yours came. I will come to you tomorrow next at 8 o'clock and will bring the Reece play with me.

With regard to the French play, I can work only from a literal translation—for, as I told you, my knowledge of the French language breaks down after ordering a dinner at a Paris restaurant. At any rate, I prefer some other person's translation of a piece to my own. When that is done I try to give an English play in place of a French one, and where I smell a foreign joke to find a good British substitute, if not equivalent. I don't think Reece's piece a bad one, of its sort, but this method is so unlike my own poor one that I fear I couldn't patch it. What *I could* try to do would be to prepare another version bringing in the best of Reece's fun. The question is—is this worth while? You, of course, have, by this time, reached the weary stage when the humour of the thing has become ghastly and revolting. To me, as yet, this isn't so—I see only the very weak female interest as a serious chance against the *great* success of the play in England.

Yrs. ever

Clement Scott, Esq. Arthur W. Pinero

Not only does this letter indicate that Pinero's work with Ohnet's *Le Maître de forges* was successful enough to elicit Scott's interest in obtaining him for the Reece play, but also Pinero's practical attitude toward the new play.

"Is it worth while?" asks the playwright who has just finished producing four plays in a single year. He was working in such a frenzy that he had time for only that work which rang the bell!

As a young bridegroom, he must have been something of a problem! Certainly he had little time for the social amenities in which Mrs. Pinero delighted. He began work at teatime and was not disturbed until the following morning, after he had partaken of breakfast in bed. That is, he did not have dinner with his family or take his wife out in the evening. He was working with monotonous regularity.

In the morning he was a human being. And guests who were invited to see him came for luncheon and to spend the early afternoon with him. But by teatime he was restless and quite unhesitant about leaving and setting to work. This rigid schedule he followed throughout his life.

His old friends could not understand this procedure. One afternoon Ellen Terry came late to Pinero's home, after a matinee. She was a favorite of Pinero, but did he wait for her? Certainly not. He was working when she arrived. Without further ado she went to look for him, promising the company that she would bring "Pin" to them. No one had ever dared to disturb him. What happened no one ever found out, but she returned without him. And his tray of sandwiches was left at his door as usual.

He always rehearsed the company before his new play was produced, and he fast acquired the reputation of being a tyrant. He cared not how distinguished the principals might be. His way was the only way, and he bellowed and snorted, requiring the repetition of some minor piece of stage business until it was done to his satisfaction. I know of no better proof which can be offered of his ability than that the most famous actors and actresses were eager to act in his plays. If he had been merely a tyrant, they would not have permitted his presumptions. He had something to give in addition to a successful play and assurance of income. Yet despite his attitude of bullying the cast into his way of doing things, individual actors and actresses have recounted in their memoirs and in interviews the high regard they had in those days for his craftsmanship.

The significance of this is not that his plays were fortunately acted by very superior companies but rather that he directed and obtained for his plays the interpretation he had in his mind when he wrote the dialogue. In other words, his genius was primarily of the stage, his knowledge of the audience's reactions, and his work for the theater, not the reader.

IV

THE COURT FARCES

THE so-called Court Farces were comedies of sentiment produced at the Court Theatre between 1885 and 1892. The writing of them came about in a curious way, but significant of Pinero's personality.

He was thirty years old and a popular playwright. He might have been content, but he was not. He knew enough about the theater to realize that he had not yet found his own technique: the individual method of writing which would stamp his plays as his own, quite different from those of any other writer. But he had written so rapidly that he had had no time to take stock of himself, to discover what he had as his own. Now he could afford to do so.

He said that he considered the temper of that day and concluded that society was essentially sentimental. He believed then, and his judgment proved to be correct, that a playwright who wished to appeal to a large audience must write plays of sentiment—light, ingenious comedies which introduced characters with ideas. This thinking then led him to emphasize foibles of character rather than faults. Instead of being cynical, he set himself to be amused by these minor errors in conduct, all of which, according to his plan, were to develop from petty ideals the sentiments of simple, naïve people.

This notion was new. He had not attempted anything of this kind before, nor had he any examples to imitate in the theater. But this was precisely the kind of material and technique to be used with great success by Barrie. In fact Barrie was writing short stories in this manner, although they were not known at the time in London.

Two old friends from his acting days, John Clayton and Arthur

Cecil, were managing the Court Theatre and eager to have something new. To them he offered *The Magistrate*. They produced it on March 21, 1885, and it ran for over three hundred performances—a new record for a London production. So prosperous was this production that when Arthur Cecil, Lottie Vance, and Mrs. Tree wished to leave for the summer, there was no difficulty at all in obtaining such celebrated players as Beerbohm Tree, Mrs. John Wood, and Marion Terry to carry on during the off-season with continued success. Pinero now found himself wealthy. And the play was translated and produced on the Continent.

64, St. John's Wood Road, N.W.
16th Decr. 1887.

Dear Scott,

I send you some extracts from the Hamburg papers referring to the production of "The Magistrate" in that city; the play has been done too in Vienna and in many other places in Germany, it seems always with success.

Perhaps you will think the matter of the connection between the English and German stages of sufficient importance for a line or two in your valuable Dramatic Notes.

The Gilbert and Sullivan Operas have already made a stand in Germany—but there you have music which is an universal language. Wyndham has triumphed over many difficulties with "David Garrick," but Davy comes to us from the French and to the French (I think) from the German. "The Magistrate," for what it is worth, is purely English and makes its way without aid of music or sensational effects of any kind. But the only importance it has in my mind is that it is the end of the wedge to open up some position for Englishmen on the German stage. The French keep us out—which considering the state of their stage just now they need not do for their own profit—and we are so busy in borrowing from the German that we forget to take our wares to Berlin. But I hope the time will come—is coming—when the Englishman like the Frenchman, will write his plays for all nations. The consciousness, when a man is writing a play, that he is working for the amusement of a few thousand middle-class English people, is not favourable to the development of Dramatic Art. That's why this German business seems of some importance—if the English writer's reach spreads, his thoughts might run out with his arm. Forgive this long scrawl.

With best regards, I am

Faithfully yrs.
Arthur Pinero

Clement Scott, Esq.

This very amusing letter reveals much of Pinero's personality. He talks of dramatic art with capitals and thinks of the greater remuneration from a larger audience. It is a young man's letter, full of pride, ambition, and the desire for more money. On the other hand, the universal appeal of *The Magistrate* marks an important development in Pinero's technique, for some present-day critics hold that eventually Pinero will be remembered for the Court Farces. Though at the moment this prophecy seems wishful thinking, in its neglect of Barrie's high attainment in this genre of sentimental comedy, the formula for these plays provides an interesting analysis; *The Magistrate* represents all of them.

It is based on the universally accepted belief that women prefer not to reveal their true ages. Mrs. Posket holds this sentiment. Upon her marriage for the second time, she lies about her own age and also about her son's. As a result, and this is the chief basis for the humor, her son is represented as fourteen when actually he is nineteen. And indeed he is a precocious lad.

The second basic assumption is the sentiment of Mr. Posket who, as a police magistrate, believes that he should be the intimate companion of his stepson and thus keep the boy out of trouble.

The complication develops from the return to England of Colonel Lukyn, who had known Mrs. Posket and her son years before in a distant post of the Empire.

Mrs. Posket must warn Colonel Lukyn not to reveal her true age, and she goes to an inn to meet him for this purpose. To this same inn, however, come Mr. Posket and his stepson. And Pinero complicates the situation by having Colonel Lukyn insist upon dining for old times' sake in the room engaged by Mr. Posket. The complication obviously inherent in this situation is heightened by the introduction of a police raid, which brings all the characters together, fortunately in the dark. Mr. Posket escapes, but the next morning in his court he is advised of his wife's predicament.

This brief analysis of the action reveals Pinero's ingenuity in plotting and the simple use of contrast in characterization; nevertheless, he has been able to hold the scene and develop from the dining-room of the inn every possible interruption which will bring confusion to his characters and their sentiments. For it is not the dialogue but the action which provides the humor. Here knowledge of stagecraft, of the practicable incidents to be presented in the theater, make the play amusing.

While *The Magistrate* was still running, he adapted Sardou's *Maison neuve* under the title of *Mayfair*. It was produced at the St. James's Theatre on October 31, 1885. But on the conclusion of *The Magistrate* he had another farce ready. *The Schoolmistress* was produced at the Court Theatre on March 27, 1886. And, like its predecessor, it too was enormously successful, following the simple formula. But before this run was finished, he established his third sentimental farce, *The Hobby Horse*, at the St. James's Theatre on October 25 of this same year. Then, upon the conclusion of the long run of *The Schoolmistress*, he had a new farce for the Court Theatre again! And there, on January 27, 1887, appeared *Dandy Dick*.

This was prolific writing and rapid wealth. And in this year another of his boyhood dreams came true. With John Hare as proposer and Squire Bancroft as seconder, he was elected to membership in the Garrick Club as a dramatic author.

But he had not forgotten Tom Robertson, the inspiration of his apprentice days. The following letter to Clement Scott indicates how he felt. This letter was written at the height of the record-breaking run of *Sweet Lavender*, produced at Terry's Theatre on March 21, 1888, and continued for 683 performances.

LONDON, 21st Octr. 1889
64, ST. JOHN'S WOOD ROAD. N.W.

DEAR SCOTT,

You may think it worthy a little note in your Friday's column that the present Mr. T. W. Robertson has just presented me with some interesting—and to me very precious relics of his father's work. They comprise printer's proof of *War*, with numerous corrections in the author's handwriting, and the written outline of a projected comedy, plans for its incidents and characters, and some notes of dialogue. Hare, Coghlan, Bancroft, and Clarke were to be provided for—but the play never went farther than this single memorandum of seven pages. Mr. Robertson gives me these remains bound in two little volumes with the inscription "To Arthur W. Pinero—a reminiscence of my father for whom he has so often expressed his admiration."

I am, Dear Scott,

Ever faithfully yours

ARTHUR W. PINERO

In other circumstances this letter might be regarded as merely Pinero's attempt for publicity, but with the Court Farces at the height of their popularity, he certainly did not need Scott's announcement. The fact is that Pinero at heart was a sentimentalist. For his overevaluation of these "remains" suggests that he had not allowed success to go to his head. Old friends too remained close to him, as the following letter reveals:

15 A GRAFTON STREET
BOND STREET WEST

DEAR PINERO

Young Webster has heard there may be some change in the cast of 'Sweet Lavender' & has asked me to write a word to you in his behalf.

I gladly do so.

He's a charming fellow whose presence on the stage is refreshing & agreeable—I'm sorry he's leaving us but there's no part for him in the next play.

Could you at any time be able to 'run him in'—he'd be very grateful I'm sure.

Sincerely yours

IRVING

28 June 1889

Again, on the completion of the run of his play at the Court Theatre, he was ready with another. *Sweet Lavender* was followed by *The Weaker Sex*. It had been tried out at the Theatre Royal in Manchester in September, 1888. It was produced in London on March 16, 1889. His audience again welcomed his latest farce.

Pinero was wise enough at this juncture to realize that some day the audience would want a change. He remembered his early play in tragic mood, *The Squire*, and set for himself the development of a new technique. For he was sensitive to the criticism now rather common that he was merely a commercial playwright.

William Archer and Edmund Gosse were lecturing about Ibsen

and translating his social plays into English. People wanted more than entertainment; theatrical audiences were becoming sophisticated enough to talk about art in the theater. And the free theaters, or subscription theaters, were successful in Christiania, Paris, and Berlin. In London, J. T. Grein, the drama critic for the Sunday edition of the *London Times*, was organizing a society for producing experimental work. For these reasons Pinero was jealous of his own place and sought to establish himself as an artist.

At just this time William S. Gilbert, the brilliant librettist and frustrated playwright, was building a new theater with the fortune derived from his share in the Gilbert and Sullivan comic operas. He had engaged John Hare, Pinero's old friend, to be the actor-manager. It was named the Garrick Theatre.

Hare asked Pinero for a play, mindful of the tremendous success Pinero had brought to the Court Theatre. And Pinero was just finishing a play, a tragedy, which he had entitled *The Profligate*. A tragedy was the last thing either Gilbert or Hare wanted; nevertheless, Pinero was the most popular playwright in London and his new play would be an auspicious opening for the Garrick Theatre.

Upon reading the play Hare was so much disturbed that he was ready to cancel the contract. The long-standing friendship was at the breaking-point. Then Hare suggested another ending, and Pinero for the first and only time in his career compromised. Some critics have made much of Pinero's acceptance of Hare's suggested ending, stating that Pinero had no high regard for his art. That judgment seems to assume that Pinero should have left his play unproduced, for its theme was too striking for any other manager to touch. It dealt with the double standard at a time when forthrightness was not a virtue; when the male could conduct himself according to his whims; but the female lost caste immediately upon the discovery of her fall, whether she was seduced or promiscuous.

Hare's position in this matter, furthermore, was perfectly justified. He was trying to establish a new theater. He was risking much even in offering an unpleasant play with a startling theme to an audience expecting another Pinero farce.

Structurally, this is the play: An innocent girl marries a profligate and then becomes the friend of a girl whom her husband had seduced. This discovery causes the bride to leave her husband. Pinero's original ending, the one retained in the printed play, revealed the husband finding his wife's hiding-place. He waits for her to return; she is delayed; he drinks poison; and she finds him dead.

Hare suggested that the husband find his wife at home, take up the glass of poison, and then dash the glass to the floor, for his wife realizes his remorse and consents to forgive him.

The idea of the double standard has faded as an exciting motive, and consequently *The Profligate* seems old fashioned. But, strikingly enough, the opposite is the case. In this play, for the first time, the conventions of the soliloquy and the aside were done away with. Pinero regarded them as artificial, as destructive of verisimilitude, as the outworn conventions of stagecraft since the days of Shakespeare.

Critics were quick to sense the importance of this development in technique, particularly from Pinero. They had begun to think of him as a clever contriver of surprises, concerned only with entertaining. Now he had revealed himself as a serious playwright, willing to risk failure in order to present an unpopular but important idea. But the success of *The Profligate* caused the critics to hesitate in their enthusiasm; perhaps, after all, Pinero had merely been clever in this instance. The change of the ending gave those who sought reassurance ample proof that Pinero was still more concerned with making money than with artistry.

Although he had done away with the unnatural devices of the soliloquy and the aside, he had accepted from the French *pièce bien faite* a device almost as difficult to accept. For O'Neill has demonstrated that even in the modern theater the soliloquy and the aside contribute to the scope of the playwright's revelations of character. People do talk when they are alone—talk to themselves and reveal their emotions. And the dramatist who avoids the use of either the soliloquy or the aside finds that he cannot very well indicate what his characters wish to keep from those with whom they talk. For the novelist can state the thoughts of his characters; the dramatist must depend upon conversation.

From the French technique Pinero took the *raisonneur*. This character explains in his dialogue precisely what the author wishes the audience to understand as his attitude toward the incidents and characters involved. In *The Profligate*, furthermore, Pinero was quite willing to accept for the climax of the plot a perfect instance of the long arm of chance; that is, he brought the wife and the seduced girl together. It might have happened in life, but life is always stranger than fiction; and in the drama such chance meetings hardly become acceptable or artistic.

William Archer, the most influential critic of the period, writing in the *World*, commended not only Hare for daring to produce the play but Pinero for expanding the scope of the drama. He even declared that the writing of this intellectual play placed Pinero as the leader of contemporary English dramatists. In the *London Times*, A. B. Walkley praised Pinero for daring to present candidly a social theme instead of continuing merely to entertain.

Pinero's pride was exalted. He sought further proof of his place in the theater, as the following letter indicates:

HIGHERCOOMBE, GRAYSWOOD, NR. HASLMERE, SURREY
29th July 1890

DEAR SCOTT,

Will you permit me to correct the statement that Mr. J. T. Grein has just arranged for the introduction of the first play of English workmanship ever produced in that country? *The Magistrate*, under its German title of *Die blaue Grotte*, has long been a popular play in all the important theatres and is at this moment in further process of adaptation into the Bohemian or Tcheco-Slavonic language for performance at the Inter-National Theatre in Prague. Whether *The Magistrate* was the first English piece done in Austria I cannot say, but I should think not.

Sweet Lavender, translated by Emil Fohl, has first seen light in Germany and will follow the same course as *Die blaue Grotte;* so also will *The Profligate* upon which the well-known Dr. Blumenthal, the literary theatrical manager of Berlin, is at work for production in the autumn. *Sweet Lavender* too is in course of translation into Italian for representation at Florence and elsewhere.

I hope you will have a pleasant and restful holiday. I have fixed myself here till the beginning of the new year, for both work and play. We are on the top of a hill with a fine view into three counties.

With kind regards, I am

Very truly yours
ARTHUR W. PINERO

Clement Scott, Esq.

Regardless of Pinero's professed interest in the new art movement of the social plays and his concern for recognition of his work translated and adapted for German and Italian audiences he had another farce ready for the management of the Court Theatre. And there on April 23, 1890, was produced *The Cabinet Minister*. His old audience was delighted. The play scored heavily. Everyone seemed relieved that his favorite playwright had given up the serious, unpleasant, problem play and had resumed the rollicking, laughter-producing incidents which turned out quite all right in the end. That is, nearly everyone; there were of course those in the audience who had hoped that Pinero would continue to present important social problems of the day.

Shortly before the première of *The Cabinet Minister*, Pinero became anxious lest his new play should not be received as the novelty he intended it to be; hence the following letter:

London, 16th Mar. 1890
64, ST. JOHN'S WOOD ROAD, N.W.

DEAR SCOTT,

I see an announcement in the Saturday papers that a new comedy by Mrs. Musgrave is to be acted at a Matinee, on April 10th, of which "the fashionable craze for aristocratic lady milliners" is the subject.

You will render me and the management of the Court Theatre a service, and not in any way prejudice the clever authoress of *Our Flat* if you will announce in your theatrical news Miss Filippi will act the character of a milliner moving in society in the play I am now rehearsing at the Court Theatre.

I will shortly send you a few particulars of my play—which has been in existence for a considerable time—if you will allow me to do so.

Sincerely yours
ARTHUR W. PINERO

Clement Scott, Esq.

This letter shows that Pinero was beginning his period of quick response to criticism. He was sensitive, insistent upon recognition, and determined to dominate the London theaters. In a word, he was conscious of new contenders for his place in the spotlight and fearful lest someone wrest from him the honors his prolific pen had won. This intensity was quite human, considering his one-track endeavor, his refusal to relax. By sheer physical strength he had forced himself to write steadily for fifteen years, and the strain was beginning to wreck his nerves.

And yet he had not begun to feel first-rate competition. Thomas Hardy had left the theater in disgust and was devoting his energy and great talent to writing novels and stories. In fact the novelists were not offering at this juncture the competition which ultimately was to overcome Pinero. The brilliant, witty dialogue of Oscar Wilde was imminent but not yet projected on the stage. Barrie was rapidly gaining a public with his novels. Shaw had just come to London to begin the long period of nine years without acceptance. Jones's melodramas were popular but limited. At thirty-five, Pinero held the control of the commercial theaters.

For these reasons he was besieged with manuscripts from authors who sought to have their plays produced. His earlier experience, however, with the disputed origin of the plot of *The Squire* made him wary of charges of plagiarism though Thomas Hardy had not pressed that case in court. Pinero refused to open any manuscript addressed to him. And this was difficult, since many distinguished literary men, perceiving his gift for adapting material to the stage, sought his aid. His aloofness aroused displeasure and criticism so that he became not only the most envied man in the theaters but the most heartily disliked.

The success of *Sweet Lavender* provides an illustration of the kind of experience with which Pinero had to contend and explains why he felt he had to remain completely out of contact with other writers.

Austin Freyers wrote a letter (dated November 29, 1890) to the editor of the influential *New Era* and charged that Pinero had

used in *Sweet Lavender* characters and incidents taken from Freyers' manuscript play, *May in December*. The following letter represents Pinero's defense.

> HIGHERCOOMBE, GRAYSWOOD
> NR. HASLEMERE, SURREY.
> 1st Dec. 1890

DEAR SCOTT,

Permit me to bring under your notice a letter signed Austin Freyers which
appeared in last Saturday's *Era*—a most mendacious attempt to discredit a
successful work.

I would ask you to forgive me for intruding upon you at such a time, but I
expect no more than that this letter will lie with many others to be dealt with
when you turn, perhaps very gladly, to work again.

> Very faithfully yours,
> ARTHUR W. PINERO

Clement Scott, Esq.

The following spring Pinero surprised critics and audiences
alike by presenting another experimental play, *Lady Bountiful*.
John Hare produced it at the Garrick Theatre on March 7, 1891,
with the principals from the cast of *The Profligate* augmented by
several notable actors. Mr. Hare played Roderick Heron, a type
which he had interpreted with great success in other Pinero plays;
Forbes-Robertson, who was later to become one of the most
popular and distinguished of Shakespearean actors both in Europe and in America, played Roderick's son; and Kate O'Rourke
played Camilla, the Lady Bountiful, torn between love for
Roderick's son and disgust with his laziness.

Robertson had used the theme years before in *Caste* and Hardy
also in his novels, but Pinero gave it new significance: the age-old
conflict between lovers from different social positions. Camilla
has wealth; Dennis lives on his father's income without knowing
that Roderick Heron receives every penny from Camilla. This
discovery sends Dennis to make his own living. And feeling sorry
for Margaret, the daughter of the riding-master for whom he
works, Dennis marries her. The conflict between their standards
of living is heightened by Dennis' discovery that Camilla loves
him. Dennis fails and Margaret becomes ill.

Meanwhile Margaret realizes that Dennis and Camilla are in love and asks Camilla to forgive her for marrying Dennis. After Margaret dies, Dennis goes away. But he returns in time to save Camilla from a loveless marriage.

More important than this manipulation of incident is Pinero's growth in power, his ability to portray women. For every turn in the plot is based upon the psychology of Camilla and Margaret. Heretofore, Pinero's feminine characters lacked intuition, sensitiveness, and depth of sentiment. And it seems likely, though Pinero himself stoutly denied my suggestion, that Ibsen's portrayal of feminine psychology influenced Pinero. However that may have been, the record clearly shows that from this time onward Pinero centered his work around women and learned to understand them so that he became the best portrayer of their whims and caprices in the twenty-year period beginning in 1890 and continuing until 1920.

Pinero's genius can hardly be denied when you consider that at thirty-five he was the idol not only of audiences but of actor-managers, wealthy, and yet at the height of his popularity ready to experiment. Had he not been a genius his tremendous energy would have been played out, for he had already written more successful plays than most men write in a lifetime. But his work of importance was yet to come.

Lady Bountiful seems old fashioned today. But the cynicism which pervades the sentimental situation was new. The critics recognized Pinero's endeavor to pierce the veil of pessimism which might easily have made this play as intense as any written by Ibsen. Walkley in the *London Times* praised Pinero for daring to experiment. But Scott of the *Daily Telegraph*, alone among all the reviewers, hit the point in describing the play as indicative of Pinero's hesitating period. That was precisely right. Pinero wished to appeal to the sentiments of his old followers of the Court Farces while at the same time he wished to win the attention of the artistic and literary critics of his day. And he failed, falling between these two objectives.

His next play, *The Times*, presented another problem arising

from class conflicts. But, unlike *Lady Bountiful*, it was satirical and
devoid of sentimentality. Its claim to present-day interest lies entirely in the circumstance that it was the first English play to be
protected under the new International Copyright Act. So at its
première at Terry's Theatre on October 24, 1891, the text of the
new play was offered for sale. Pinero's excitement about this new
opportunity appears in the following letter.

LONDON, 21st Septr. 1891
64 ST. JOHN'S WOOD ROAD, N.W.

MY DEAR MR. SCOTT,

   I wish I had known that your Dramatic Column was to have made so early
an appearance; a fortnight ago, on making enquiries about it, I was told that
you did not start the gossip until Octr. I fear I have now nothing that is new to
say in reference to my play which is to be done at Terry's Theatre, save that
although it has been announced for the 10th of Octr. the date of production is
more likely to be the 17th of that month. The cast has already been published.
The piece will be described as a comedy but it may perhaps be found to lean
more to the side of satire than sentiment.

   I hope you will consider it worth some little comment that I intend on the
first night of *The Times*, and at the subsequent performances, to offer the book of
the play to the public. It will be the first of the series of my pieces which Mr.
William Heinemann is about to publish in monthly installments. *The Profligate*
will form the second vol; and very likely, *The Cabinet Minister* the third. Since
Macready's time (we remember the way in which *The Blot on the 'Scutcheon* was
hurried through the press so that it might be ready for the production) such a
thing as publishing a new dramatic work as an accompaniment to its first representation has not, I think, occurred.

   With all good wishes, I am

Sincerely yours
ARTHUR W. PINERO

Clement Scott, Esq.

   Publication of his plays, however, was to reveal to the public
that Pinero's dialogue on the printed page did not have the
validity it possessed in the theater. And Pinero never learned the
art of writing stage directions and descriptions of characters to
stimulate the imagination of the average reader. Both Barrie and
Shaw were to gain a wide following from their printed plays, but
they described the scenes, the action, and the costumes of their
characters and did not hesitate to explain to their readers pre-

cisely what was going to happen. Pinero simply printed the directions of use on the stage but made no attempt to re-create what the stage actually supplied to the theatrical audience. In other words, this event which he hailed with such evident delight was to become the basis for the eventual decline of his reputation as a dramatist.

Within this period from 1885 to 1891 Pinero wrote more than a dozen plays, four in one year, to win fame and fortune. But had he quit in 1891, at the age of thirty-six, there would have been no justification to write a book about him. For to this point in his career, despite the popularity of his plays and the wealth they had earned him, he had not written for posterity; he was only a remarkably successful writer for the commercial theater.

In 1891 he began work on *The Second Mrs. Tanqueray*, the play which was tantamount to revolution in the London theaters. He had found himself after twelve years of constant writing and now was to experience twenty full years of major achievement.

V

THE SECOND MRS. TANQUERAY

IN THE autumn of 1891 Pinero began writing *The Second Mrs. Tanqueray*. Again, as in *The Profligate*, he was concerned with the social problems arising from the double standard of morality. But now he reversed the plot motive; instead of the husband's past confronting the wife, the wife's past was to bring grief to the husband; instead of this situation coming as a surprise, a chance discovery, the husband in the new play was to know about his wife's past and hope that disillusionment would not come. This new attitude was considerably advanced, for the wife in *The Profligate* was rather naïve and so innocent that disillusionment might be expected. But the husband in *The Second Mrs. Tanqueray* was to be a man of the world, determined to prove the moral prejudices of society quite wrong.

Pinero worked on this play longer and with more careful consideration of the theme than he had ever given to a play before. But when he finished the script, though he was at the height of his popularity, John Hare rejected it. Not for years had he had difficulty with actor-managers, except in the instance of Hare's opening a new theater with *The Profligate*. Pinero had written *The Second Mrs. Tanqueray* with John Hare and Forbes-Robertson in mind for the two leading roles. He had assumed that the success of *The Profligate*, which vindicated his belief in the readiness of London audiences to receive unpleasant material, would encourage Hare to continue experimenting.

But Hare flatly refused. Pinero argued, to no end. Then, in a huff, he left his old friend and began the tedious search for a producer. The fact that Hare had refused the manuscript made other managers wary. And Pinero, who had never had to peddle his wares, became heartily bitter as he received one rejection after another. In particular, he wanted George Alexander, the young, promising actor-manager of the St. James's Theatre, to take a chance. But Alexander, who was then producing Oscar Wilde's *Lady Windermere's Fan*, had a witty, social play which was rapidly becoming the talk of the town. Alexander, furthermore, was afraid that Pinero's play would be too shocking for good taste, too frank to be popular.

Finally Pinero prevailed to the extent that Alexander was willing to try the play in special matinee performances. Pinero was more than grateful and quickly dispatched the following letter.

LONDON, 29 OCTR. 1892
70 A, HAMILTON TERRACE, N.W.

DEAR SCOTT,

In tomorrow's paper Mr. George Alexander announces a play of my writing for production at his theatre during the season.

This play, on which I have long been engaged, has a modern setting but its interest is of an entirely serious kind. It is in four acts and called *The Second Mrs. Tanqueray*.

I am, Dear Scott,

Yours very truly,

ARTHUR W. PINERO

Clement Scott Esq.

But, alas, Pinero was doomed to disappointment. For the production was delayed month after month, while in vain Alexander tried to obtain a prominent actress for the role of Paula. None of them wished to risk their reputations in the part. And, in addition, Wilde's play continued to hold the attention of playgoers.

On March 7, 1893, Pinero saw the première of another Court Farce, *The Amazons*, while still waiting for Alexander to produce the masterpiece. *The Amazons* was a lighthearted and ridiculous extravaganza based on a mother's dressing her three daughters as boys and so bringing them up to please their father. This misrepresentation of their sex obviously cast every scene in the humor of dramatic irony. This comedy was well received; the old Court audience had long been neglected and responded with bravos.

Finally Alexander persuaded a little-known but brilliant young actress, Mrs. Pat Campbell, to play Paula. But at the close of the season Alexander suddenly decided to give the new play, in which he would play Tanqueray, a complete trial, not merely at matinees. This was the chance for which Pinero had been striving for over a year, although the première on May 27, 1893, was rather late for a long run. Neither Pinero nor Alexander expected commercial success; they hoped for understanding and appreciation of the play. They received everything!

The critics seemed to contend with one another in the search for superlatives with which to express their delight. Walkley in the *Times* proudly compared the new English play with Dumas' *La Dame aux camélias* and Augier's *Le Mariage d'Olympe*, which were highly regarded at the moment. Scott in the *Daily Telegraph* gave his reasons for considering Pinero's play superior to Ibsen's *Ghosts*, which the Stage Society had recently performed in London. William Archer declared that Paula was one of the finest acting roles ever created! He added that the commercial theater in London had with this play attained the artistic level of M. Antoine's Théâtre libre in Paris. In other words, Pinero's period of frustration had turned out rather well. And now to analyze the play.

The first act is a model of perfect technique. When the curtain rises, the audience' curiosity is immediately aroused. Three gentlemen are seated at the dinner table, but the fourth chair, the one toward the audience, is vacant. Where is the absentee? Why isn't he there? Who is he? Tanqueray tells his guests that he is sorry Cayley Drummle hasn't come because this is a farewell dinner. He is going to marry a woman with a past, whom their wives will not accept. Thus are established three story leads: (1) the question of Cayley Drummle; (2) the question of Tanqueray's marriage; and (3) the question of society's attitude toward the woman he loves.

The author is now free to develop the situation, assured of the audience' aroused curiosity and interest. And all this has been accomplished before the curtain has been up three minutes!

Then Cayley Drummle bustles into the room and unintentionally says what hurts Tanqueray most. Why, asks Drummle, do men of property marry notorious women? Of course Drummle does not know that this is precisely what Tanqueray proposes to do, for he has been delayed, reconciling Lady Orreyed to her son's marriage.

Soon the other guests leave. Tanqueray explains to Drummle that he believes it is possible to rear a life of happiness upon a miserable foundation. And this idea, or rather the disproof of it, becomes the theme of the play. The disillusionment of Tanqueray is the heart of the tragedy to unfold.

When Drummle leaves, Paula enters. Her coming to Tanqueray's bachelor apartments in the late Victorian period stamped her as a careless woman. (That is a situation now lost to the modern audience.) She gives Tanqueray some letters which tell all about her past. He throws them into the fire. Then she declares that if he ever stopped loving her, she would destroy herself.

When Paula leaves, Tanqueray finds on the mantelpiece a letter from Ellean, the teen-aged daughter of his first wife. Ellean, who had planned to enter the convent in Paris, is coming home to keep house for him, not knowing of his intention to marry again. Curtain!

There are the problems. Can Tanqueray bring together, to mutual understanding, these two girls: his covent-bred daughter and the notorious woman he will marry? Is his love for Paula so great that he can, as he proposes, give up his old friends? Can Paula and Tanqueray find happiness together despite society's readiness to remember her past? Will Paula's past complicate Tanqueray's happiness?

In the second act all of these questions are answered in the negative. In the third act Paula and Ellean arrive at an understanding only to have Ellean discover that her fiancé once kept house with Paula. Whereupon Paula, without the love of Ellean and Tanqueray, destroys herself.

The ending has been called melodramatic. But it is motivated in Act I by Paula's declaration to Tanqueray, when both were optimistic.

Shaw, some years later, took exception to the waste of Mr. Misquith and Dr. Jayne, who are guests at Tanqueray's dinner party but do not reappear in the play. But the audience cannot forget their absence; that is the point. Their wives will not accept Paula, just as Tanqueray suspected. In other words, what Shaw called waste is actually one of the most subtle bits of dramaturgy on record. But Shaw's remarks should not be taken seriously, except that many unthinking critics have copied them. Shaw was frustrated and hungry at the time, the author of unpublished novels, stories, and plays. Everyone was praising Pinero's play, and it was a typical and characteristic Shavian procedure to pick a flaw in it. The pity is that anyone believed Shaw meant it.

Today, authors avoid presentation of abstract moral problems and emphasize specific situations: unemployment, poor housing, working conditions, social diseases, and juvenile delinquencies. The rise of the proletariat, the struggle of the bourgeois, and the decline of aristocracy—these are the problems of our time. Since the first World War, new standards of morality, at least the acceptance of a single standard of morality and the denial of responsibility, have amounted to social revolution. Hence the double standard of morality seems at the moment to continue—as it has for the last twenty years—merely an academic interest.

Fundamentally, however, the chief conflicts of society have developed from the struggle for power and survival; it is only a matter of emphasis and point of view when the modern critic deplores the use of the double standard as a theme in the drama. It is, in fact, the difference between the treatment of the problem in *The Profligate* and that of *The Second Mrs. Tanqueray;* the disparity between naïveté and urbanity; between the discovery of evil in the world and the search for happiness despite evil.

The test of a play's importance is determined by its success in the theater. *The Second Mrs. Tanqueray* has been produced in revival more times than any other modern English play and more widely translated. But the proof of its supremacy as an acting play lies in the record of the great actresses who have played Paula: in particular, the incomparable Eleanora Duse. But in the London theaters the list is a long one: Mrs. Pat Campbell played in a revival in 1901, with George Arliss and Gerald du Maurier playing the male leads. Later, Miss Olga Nethersole, Miss Granville, and Miss Gladys Cooper all scored heavily in the role. In America, Mrs. Kendall encountered severe criticism; her public was scandalized that she would appear as a prostitute. But later, in 1924–25, Ethel Barrymore achieved success not only in New York but on tour of the more conventional midland cities. And the recent and favorable reception accorded the play in the summer theaters leads to the hope that Tallulah Bankhead will soon appear on Broadway in the role of Paula.

If *The Second Mrs. Tanqueray* is not a masterpiece, as some modern critics would believe, then their view is myopic. For they have failed to distinguish between plays for the theater and plays for the reader, between *Julius Caesar* and *King Lear*, in their demand for *Hamlet*. For it is not the idea in *The Second Mrs. Tanqueray* that is important, but the execution of it in practicable acting roles.

Tanqueray's desire to forget Paula's past is not a profound thought, but the desire to overcome obstacles of birth, education, old faults, and mistakes is universal. That desire the audience shares with the characters, however unimportant or old fashioned the moral issue may appear.

Pinero had finally hit upon a formula which he was to develop repeatedly during the next eighteen years, each time to the satisfaction of his audience. Of course it is pleasant to assume today our superiority to the London audiences and the critics from 1892 to 1909. In fact, it is flattering for some of us to point out that a work of art in the theater should not be judged on the basis of its appeal at the box office. That is, however, the easiest point to make and the most invalid; namely, that the people are always wrong; the critic, right. It can be demonstrated that Pinero developed from the days of *The Money Spinner* in 1880. And if *The Second Mrs. Tanqueray* and the plays which followed it are demon-

St. James's

KING STREET, ST. JAMES'S, S.W.

Theatre

Sole Lessee and Manager - SIR GEORGE ALEXANDER

George Alexander

GENERAL MANAGER - - CHARLES T. H'T HELMSLEY

(To whom all communications should be addressed)

Stage Manager:	Treasurer:	Musical Director:
E. Vivian Reynolds	D. W. Whitaker	William Robins
Secretary:	Box Office Manager:	Assistant Stage Manager:
A. P. Borne	E. Arnold	Percy D. Owen

49

This Evening, Wednesday, June 4th, 1913, at 8.15

WILL BE REVIVED

THE SECOND
MRS. TANQUERAY

A Play, In Four Acts,

By ARTHUR PINERO

Aubrey Tanqueray	GEORGE ALEXANDER (His Original Character)
Sir George Orreyed, Bart.	JAMES LINDSAY
Captain Hugh Ardale	REGINALD MALCOLM
Cayley Drummle	NIGEL PLAYFAIR
Frank Misquith, Q.C., M.P.	A. E. BENEDICT
Gordon Jayne, M.D.	E. VIVIAN REYNOLDS
Morse	FRANK G. BAYLY
Servants at "Highercoombe"	JOHN RIDLEY MARY CLARE
Lady Orreyed	LETTICE FAIRFAX
Mrs. Cortelyon	KATE BISHOP
Paula	Mrs. PATRICK CAMPBELL (Her Original Character)
Ellean	ROSALIE TOLLER

The Scene of the First Act is laid at Mr. Tanqueray's Rooms, No. 2x, The Albany, in the month of November; the occurrences of the succeeding Acts take place at his house, "Highercoombe," near Willowmere, Surrey, during the early part of the following year.

50

Programme of Music.

OVERTURE	...	...	...	"Orphée aux Enfers"	...	...	...	*Offenbach*
FANTASIE	...	...	...	"Hongroise."	...	...	...	*Michaels*
BALLET	...	...	...	"Coppélia"	...	...	...	*Délibes*
POTPOURRI	...	...	...	"Melodious Memories"	...	...	...	*Finch*
MARCHE	...	...	...	"Tzigane" ...	...	...	...	*Lacome*

MATINEE EVERY WEDNESDAY at 2.15

PRICES:

Private Boxes, £4 4s. Stalls, 10/6 Dress Circle, 7/6 Upper Circle, Front Row, 5/- Other Rows, 4/-
Pit, 2/6 Gallery, 1/-

Box-Office (E. ARNOLD) Open 10 till 10. Seats can be booked by Letter,
Telegram ("Ruritania, St. James's, London") or Telephone No. 3903 Gerrard).

Machinist, J. CULLEN. Chief Engineer, EDWARD MOREHEN. Property Master, W. DAVIES.
Wardrobe Mistress, Mrs. EVANS.

This Theatre is so well provided with exits, that every member of the audience can, without hurry,
get clear of the Auditorium within TWO MINUTES.

The Scenery in this Theatre has been rendered Fire-proof by the NON-FLAMMABLE WOOD FABRICS Co. Ltd.

Extract from the Rules made by the Lord Chamberlain.

(1) The name of the actual and responsible Manager of the Theatre must be printed on every play bill. (2) The Public can leave the Theatre at the end of the performance by all exit and entrance doors, which must open outwards. (3) Where there is a fireproof screen to the proscenium opening it must be lowered at least once during every performance to ensure its being in proper working order. (4) Smoking is not permitted in the auditorium. (5) All gangways, passages and staircases must be kept free from chairs or any other obstructions, whether permanent or temporary.

strably superior in technique, then their success at the box office must indicate the rise of sophistication among playgoers.

Pinero was not an unsuccessful playwright who suddenly scored a box-office hit and as a result that hit became a masterpiece. The long period of his continued popularity as well as his remarkable development should be considered before his work is lightly discarded, if only discarded by the critic unprepared to take the long view.

VI

FURTHER EXPERIMENTATION

MORE important than the fact that *The Second Mrs. Tanqueray* actually earned more than $150,000 for Pinero, a considerable amount from royalties in the 1890's, was Pinero's discovery of his métier—the dramatization of marriage problems. For Paula was his first feminine character of any significance. His heroines heretofore had been puppets; they fitted into the plot schemes; they certainly did not appear to think for themselves or to be motivated in their speech and actions by the whims of the eternal feminine!

Pinero had at last discovered that women are motivated to speak and act quite differently from men. And he had also learned how to create a man with ideals in sharp contrast to the roués and weaklings he had previously created. The tolerance and liberality of Cayley Drummle made of him more than stock type from French drama, the *raisonneur*. In writing *The Second Mrs. Tanqueray*, Pinero had discovered three important characters: the luxury-loving woman, the man who could understand and sympathize with her, and the clever liberal. These he was to re-use in subsequent plays. Regardless of how he changed the plot situation, these three characters form the basis for his new system.

Undoubtedly Pinero's willingness to accept a formula for his social plays, even as he had for the Court Farces, led critics to condemn him—to describe his work as merely commercial. That was Pinero's weakness. Even now that he had no reason to fear poverty, he still wanted to write successful plays—successful at the box office. But that seems a perfectly natural attitude, except

53

among artists. Yet of course there are many instances of artists who wrote for posterity only to be damned.

Pinero did choose to travel and to see life outside of the theater. That was a great change. In his career to this point he had been the observer rather than the participant. He had looked through the window into the drawing-room without entering and observing for himself. He had in fact been too willing to accept the theatrical version of life as life.

Pinero had vindicated his position as a dramatist. *Lady Bountiful*, *The Profligate*, and *The Second Mrs. Tanqueray* showed his contemporaries that he was striving to raise the standard for theatrical entertainment in London. It is easy today to forget how low the standards were then and how much courage it required to write seriously for the theater. Ibsen's plays were misunderstood and criticized unmercifully, despite the endeavors of Edmund Gosse and William Archer to interpret what Ibsen had to say. Both of these men were as close to Pinero as anyone could be. He respected their opinions; he wanted them to respect his plays. But he was writing for the London theaters, not for Antoine's Théâtre libre in Paris. Pinero actually believed that he was performing at that time a great service, though he did not write about his opinions.

Henry Arthur Jones, however, became so imbued with the new plays of moral protest that he devoted half his time to writing articles and delivering lectures. He finally wrote a book, *The Renascence of the English Drama*, to arouse the English public, to make playgoers realize what exciting times were theirs in the development of the English drama. Jones later realized that his missionary work was to no avail. Only through plays can the public be brought to appreciate better plays.

Pinero's sensitiveness about his artistic reputation had increased with his wealth and power. He became abnormally jealous of his position, arrogant, but at the same time eager for praise. This human side of the skilful playwright led him to defend his work unnecessarily, as the following letter indicates:

40 QUEEN SQUARE
30 November, 94

MY DEAR PINERO,

Your two letters reached me together this morning, but I happened to read them in the order in which they were written so can assure you that I was in no way hurt by the phrase about Ibsen, & did not read it at all as a sneer. I don't think there is any misunderstanding between us as to the municipal theatres— only a difference of opinion on the purely abstract question of their desirability. Of one thing you may be sure—the first muncipality that seriously thinks of building a theatre will be so utterly different from any existing muncipality that no argument based on the existing municipalities can properly apply to it. In other words, as I said before, the argument is as yet wholly in the air.

But even from your own point of view, I don't think you should be so contemptuous of your friends the architects. Suppose they do hanker after the building of beautiful theatres, is that any more condemnable than your own hankering after the writing of worthy plays. A theatre ought to be one of the most beautiful of possible buildings—& until a very few years ago there wasn't a theatre in England, except Covent Garden, that hadn't the aspect of a third-rate gin-palace. Architects, I take it, are in this country even more defrauded of their due opportunities than dramatists are or used to be, & they'd be poor creatures indeed if they didn't prick up their ears at the suggestion of a revival of theatre-building. Don't you yourself, when you go abroad & find in town after town the theatre a magnificent structure occupying the best site in the city—don't you yourself feel that the drama gains enormously in consideration from the mere fact of its physical recognition, so to speak, among the public institutions of the country? Believe me, the calling in of the architect will be one of the first steps towards the final demolition of the Puritan prejudice against the drama. But I don't think you need be in the least afraid that it will be the municipalities that will first call him in. As to the social status of the actor, I don't precisely know what you mean. The only country in which I have any personal knowledge as to the social status of the actor is Denmark, where the theatre had been a state institution for centuries, & there the actor's position is all that can possibly be desired. So it is, I understand, in Germany; & I don't see that they have very much to complain of in France. It is true Universities don't ask them to deliver lectures—there is not much, perhaps, of the actor-mania which in England seems to me rather degrading than otherwise to the profession—but I don't think they lack any reasonable social consideration. With actresses, in France, the case is somewhat different, but is not because the theatres are endowed, but because the French actress is still very apt to live up to her traditional reputation.

As to the Ibsen play, it is very good of you to take an interest in the matter, but I'm afraid this one is hopeless from the ordinary managerial point of view. In the first place, I don't believe Pigott will license it; in the second place it is so painful that I don't think it could possibly become *popular*. This between ourselves—I mustn't, of course, prejudice the play's chances, such as they are. I should think twice about going to see it myself. The second act seems to me to be one of the most intolerably agonizing things that ever were written. At the same time, its technical adaptation to the stage is to my mind marvelous, so I suppose it's bound to be done. The matter, of course, is not in my hands but in Heinemann's—but, acting simply in Ibsen's interests, I should strongly advise him to have nothing to do with the actor-managers in the matter. There is one of them who I am sure would give his eyes for the piece, even if he could only do it at a private performance; but I'd *much* rather see it land on the shelf altogether than entrusted to him. You know I have never agreed with you on this "side-show" question, especially as concerns Ibsen. Why *should* Ibsen be popular? What possibility is there of his ever becoming so—except perhaps some of his earlier plays, that do not depart from the ordinary Franco-English formula of construction? What translated (not adapted) dramatist ever was popular in a foreign country, except Shakespeare in Germany & Mr. Brandon Thomas all the world over—& even *Charley's Aunt* is adapted? What is the good of trying to force caviar in shovel-fulls down the throats of the general. Nothing is more inconceivable to me than a big monetary success for any of his later plays—& there are few things I care less about. Ibsen appeals to a small public within the great public—& he affects the great public through them, through you, through me, through everyone whom he shakes out of the old ruts—but certainly not in our time to the extent of making himself popular. I believe—& I have seen something of what I speak about—that Ibsen has on the whole done nowhere better than here—in the side shows—precisely because he was handled by people whose first thought was to interpret him faithfully. Abroad, where he is taken up by the ordinary impresario in the ordinary way of business, & played by artists who would probably prefer to be playing *Charley's Aunt*, he is ever apt to be murdered—as he was at the one actor-manager theatre where he has been done here. For my part I don't want a better performance than that of the *Master Builder* at the Trafalgar Square. I remember you said I had made a mistake in giving the figures of Ibsen's receipts in an article I wrote last year, but I think you mistook my purpose. I hadn't the least intention of showing that Ibsen was popular. All I wanted to show, & I believe did show, was that it was absurd to pretend that nobody went to see his plays—that, in fact, he had a paying public, though a small one. The purpose of the article was to bring to a focus the ridiculous nonsense that has been written about Ibsen by the critics, & the assertion that no one could be bribed to sit out his plays was one of their favorite idiocies.

I'm afraid this is a very ungracious return for your very kind offer of help, which, believe me, I appreciate none the less. Perhaps I may come upon you after all for advice or assistance if I have anything to do with the staging of the new play. In the meantime, I'm off to Cambridge to a side-show there—Euripides this time, not Ibsen. Please don't let Miss Myra see this letter, even in the distance—my typewriter has forfeited all title to my esteem.

Yours ever

WILLIAM ARCHER

This important letter deals with many significant problems in the London theaters, but in particular with the insular attitude of Englishmen in their refusal to accept Ibsen's plays. Here may be seen good reason why Pinero was always annoyed by the critics who insisted that he owed much to Ibsen's plays. Pinero did not regard Ibsen as highly as did Archer, but even Archer found Ibsen's work uneven and objected to the pervading gloom.

Two years after the première of *The Second Mrs. Tanqueray*, Pinero finished *The Notorious Mrs. Ebbsmith*. Meanwhile, Alexander had accepted Jones's *The Masqueraders* for the St. James's Theatre. So Pinero turned to John Hare, who had refused to produce *The Second Mrs. Tanqueray* but who, since its phenomenal success, had been eager to have another Pinero play.

The Notorious Mrs. Ebbsmith was performed at the Garrick Theatre on March 13, 1895, with Mrs. Pat Campbell, who had created Paula, in the role of Agnes Ebbsmith. Forbes-Robertson, for whom the part of Tanqueray had been written, played Lucas Cleeve, a weak but lovable young aristocrat, with whom Agnes falls in love despite the fact that young Cleeve has a wife. Hare took the part of the Duke of St. Olpherts, an unprincipled character of the type Pinero had created for this actor many times before. But in this play the Duke was not merely a type but a clever, evil person motivated by a good reason, judged by Victorian standards.

Again Pinero was dealing with the ethical good and bad involved in the principle that the end justifies the means. But in comparison with Victorian standards Pinero's thinking was liberal and, in the opinion of many of his contemporaries, apparently too advanced. Why present-day critics should select this par-

ticular aspect of Pinero's thinking and condemn him as conserva-
tive may well be questioned. Pinero was not concerned with any
system of ethics popular among the leaders of his time. Undefined
though they seem, success and happiness as the ultimate reward
are the principles for conduct indicated in his plays.

Agnes, like Paula, had an unfortunate past, but in a different
way. Agnes found disillusionment in marriage; consequently she
seeks happiness outside of marriage, in direct contrast to Paula's
search for happiness in marriage. When Agnes, having risked her
reputation and sacrificed herself for Lucas, realizes that she is
losing him, she tries to find solace in religion. But in despair she
hurls her Bible into the stove; then snatches it from the flames.
Public indignation over this scene was so great that Pinero described the book as "a small leather-bound book" in the printed
version of the play.

This sensational incident doubtless brought many people to the
theater, for the play was widely discussed. Shaw's *Mrs. Warren's
Profession* a few years later caused as much excitement; in fact, it
was closed by order of the censor. But both plays had more merit
than was perceived by the average playgoer.

Agnes Ebbsmith was not notorious; she seemed notorious when
viewed from false standards. She had the strength of Ibsen's great
heroine, Hedda Gabler. And Pinero reveals the source of her
strength. It is protest—protest against the false standards of society. She began life amid poverty, following her father in the
calling of street-corner preacher. Then she married and had her
ideals destroyed. But she found in young Cleeve an intellectual
companion, while she nursed him back to health. Then, despite
all her idealism, she fell in love with him and strove to hold him at
any sacrifice.

This change from intellectual to physical relationship is contra-
dictory to her principles of idealistic companionship rather than
sensual pleasure. And she fails even then because opposed to her
stands the Duke of St. Olphert, a shrewd rationalist, who reminds
his nephew of the husband's duty to cleave unto his wife. This is
sound morality provided that theirs is mutual love and respect.
Such is not the situation; neither Cleeve nor his wife wishes to do

more than maintain a hypocritical front for respectability—a
theme which Pinero took from Browning's well-known short
poem.

Among the contemporary reviewers both Archer and Walkley
praised this noticeable advance in Pinero's ability to delineate his
heroine. One critic, however, found the play "monotonously
squalid and slow." Pinero had discovered that emphasis upon
character leaves less opportunity for skilful manipulation of plot;
that is, when the playwright creates lifelike characters, the characters cannot be easily forced into a deftly manipulated plot.
The choice lies between delineation of characters and quick-mov-
ing incidents.

When the Garrick Club, a few months later, gave a testimonial
dinner in honor of Sir Henry Irving, Pinero was asked to give the
principal address. Heretofore he had avoided public appearances
outside the theater. Here is Irving's note in appreciation:

LYCEUM THEATRE

MY DEAR PINERO

I must write to thank you for the most beautiful address today—which
touched me to the heart.

Thanks and thanks again old friend, I shall never forget it.

Sincerely ever

HENRY IRVING

19 July 1895

Seven months after the première of *The Notorious Mrs. Ebbsmith*,
Pinero watched the opening night of *The Benefit of the Doubt* at the
Comedy Theatre, on October 16, 1895. This play he had written
rapidly, as if to meet the declining interest in *The Notorious Mrs.
Ebbsmith* and keep a Pinero play on the London stage. But *The
Benefit of the Doubt* met failure chiefly because he was again striving to please the audience who liked his comedies and also the
group interested in social problems; with this play he satisfied
neither group.

The formula is the new one, centered around the misunderstood woman. But Theo has only that characteristic in common
with Paula and Agnes. Theo is named the correspondent in divorce proceedings brought by John Allington's wife. The evi-

dence is inconclusive, and the judge, after lecturing her, gives her the benefit of the doubt.

Pinero attempted to show that scandal can involve innocent women who are careless of public opinion. Such was Theo. The difficulty for the audience lay in Pinero's treatment. He was not decisive in sketching her character. In her speech and actions she is free and frivolous, the kind of woman likely to have an affair with Allington. Her innocence rests solely on Allington's testimony and his desire to be rid of her.

In *The Benefit of the Doubt*, Pinero had taken a serious subject and treated it lightly but had failed to make clear to the audience what should be the response. The lighthearted thought it was an unpleasant play; the serious-minded regarded Pinero's manner as flippant. Archer, Walkley, and Shaw praised the craftsmanship in creating verisimilitude, but the critic in the *Era* made articulate the public's reaction: "Is he sneering in his sleeve at the decadent and debased society he depicts; or is he in sympathy with it?" The answer is that Pinero loathed society but was dependent upon it for the support of his plays.

He did not offer another play until a year and a half later. He traveled widely, went to the theater, and tried to recapture his point of view on society. One night at the Lyceum Theatre he observed an awkward bit of stage business and wrote to Sir Henry about it. Irving's reply is important because it indicates Pinero's position in the London theaters.

15 A GRAFTON STREET
BOND STREET W.

MY DEAR PINERO

I was delighted to get your letter & my hearty thanks are yours for the admirable suggestion which I have put into practice greatly.— & certainly to the advantage of the performance

It is a 'funny' play isn't it?—& I was glad when I found that it had engaged your practical interest in our stage manoeuvres—but if I am "Sir Henry" any more, I shall have to address you, old friend, as Field Marshal

Sincerely always

HENRY IRVING

10 Oct 1896

Irving was not the person to flatter, particularly a playwright who had offered his plays to others and had made fortunes for rival managers. But Irving was above petty jealousy and ready to accept his younger friend's suggestions. This is certain, however: few persons would have dared to show Irving how to improve the stage business in one of his productions. Irving was a master of productions, but Pinero had come a long way.

Pinero's conceit was now at full tide. He was hard at work on a new comedy, ready to give his public what it wanted and abandon the problem plays. When he finished *The Princess and the Butterfly*, he sent the manuscript to George Alexander and received the following letter in reply:

> VICARAGE COTTAGE
> OVINGDEEN DE.
> Dece. 21, 96

MY DEAR P.

I hope you got my brief wire of delight on reading the play. It is wonderful, —simply wonderful, and exceeds my highest hopes. Interesting—absorbingly interesting, especially in the last three acts. That fourth act—for direct humanity, perfection of workmanship and sheer brilliancy of intellectuality and power equals anything you have ever done.

The last act, too, is startling in its genius, with its manipulation of "the fairy tale, happy for ever after" ending—it fairly takes one's breath away, it is so delicate, so profound and so limitlessly human in its analysis. Do you care to come here with me for a Sunday in January? If so I shall be delighted any Sunday except the 17th.

I've seen Zelbin & arranged with him for the last scene he will have the model done early in Jany. when I'll get you to look at it. My good wishes to Mrs. Pin & yourself; we are here till Friday

> Yours
>
> ALEC

This is the sheerest piece of critical nonsense ever written. Whether Alexander meant it or not, the play was regarded as fluff; and there is no reason to change or to attempt to change the contemporary estimate. It did, however, reveal Pinero's versatility, for it was as unlike anything he had previously attempted as could be imagined. Pinero's style was not suited to light dialogue.

The Princess and the Butterfly was produced at the St. James's Theatre on March 29, 1897.

Pinero returned to his earlier strain of deep sentiment for his next play. Obviously he was experimenting now, quite uncertain of what to write. But, even though the critics were generous, experimentation was not enough.

Trelawny of the "Wells" was produced successfully at the Court Theatre on January 20, 1898. It appealed directly to the sentimentalists. Tom Wrench, the leading character, represented Tom Robertson; thus Pinero felt he was paying a debt for all that Robertson had indirectly taught him about playwriting. The critics of course saw this point and praised the author for the generous tribute. As a novelty, likewise, this first introduction of backstage life and the greenroom made a hit. But intellectually, this play reveals the depth of Pinero's decline. He was content to depend upon sentimentality rather than ideas to carry the development of the plot.

The basic conflict, the misunderstanding between society and actors, was an old Robertsonian theme. Rose Trelawny discovers that she cannot find happiness outside her class; she was born to the theater, not in society. But her brief stay with her fiancé's family stimulates her ambition; she is not content to remain as an entertainer at the Wells. She finds happiness when her fiancé produces Tom's queer play, with an opportunity thus provided for her to become a popular actress.

Here was the happy ending the audience wanted, as well as sweet sadness. During 1927 John Drew, with an all-star cast, toured America with this play. This was at the time when *Abie's Irish Rose* was at its height. Folksy plays with direct appeal to tears that can be brushed aside and illumined with laughter at the end never fail to charm the naïve.

Meanwhile Pinero's phenomenal success completely overcame the impetuous Ellen Terry, who had tried for several years to bring her husband and Pinero together again. Here is a letter which she dashed off, suffused with emphasis expressed in her handwriting.

DEAR MR. PINNY—

Whenever I ask "the Governor" about Pinny's plan for the Lyceum he wrinkles up the sides of his forehead, his eyebrows fly to nearly the top of his head, he sighs, looks frightfully worried, & then of course one feels a coward to go on with the attack—Oh Lord, Oh Lord, *do* please let me have the enormous pleasure of seeing him act a play of yours there at the Lyceum. Why not? *Is it me?* Am *I* the too old woman who hinders—? But one can 'specially engage anyone,' you know— For pity's sake don't think you can hurt my feelings (except by not writing a lovely modern play for Henry—) I'll do anything you think I can do—I'll help in any way. I wonder & wonder—often & often why you just leave us out in the cold—Don't think for a moment that Henry w^d be wanting to stage manage a play of yours if you w^d DO IT FOR HIM.—I think at times c^d that account for—But how silly. You are both big men so no fear—But still *Why?*— *Why?*—I've been dreadfully ill with my first "Flu"!—& stuck here at Margate in bed—the whole of the last fortnight—Never before have I known what it is to be *bored*—*Oh*—*how dreadful!* Forgive me boring *you*, & do give me one line of comfort & say you'll write a Duck of a Play—*Modern*—(the scene *out of doors* if possible) for the Lyceum with a shrewd loveable man in it for Henry—& if I can come in usefully (& brightly) so much the better—My *purpose* in writing to you is serious although I can't word it properly—

Dear Pinny I hope you are well & that you may never *never* have *the Flu!*

Yrs always
ELLEN TERRY

1—PARAGON—MARGATE
    8—March

In reply Pinero wrote directly to Irving and offered to write a play for him. Irving replied as follows:

THE BATH HOTEL
BOURNEMOUTH

MY DEAR PINERO

How good you are & how truly kind is your suggestion.

Such a help as yours would under some conditions be of inestimable value— but my present intention is to produce no more new work at the Lyceum—certainly not for some time—but to travel—to realise & not to speculate.

This with health & strength I can easily do.

I am quite well again, but have promised not to work for some little time—& to get all the rest & sunshine I can.

The rest is a bore—but the sunshine here is beautiful & has been for the last two days intense.

If you should ever be drifting this way what a delight it would be to see you— but I know how busy you are—at least I have Hare's authority for that statement.

But I should much like to see you & if not before when I get to town again, we must get together.

Indeed, old fellow, believe me, my heart is full of your kindness. I feel it deeply & with love

Am ever yrs.

HENRY IRVING

20 Dec 1898

In 1899 Pinero was elected to the General Committee of the Garrick Club. During the two years since the première of *The Princess and the Butterfly*, his plays were produced by various managers but not by Alexander. In reply to Pinero's overture for resumption of their old friendship, Alexander wrote as follows:

CROMER

Aug 11, 1899

MY DEAR P.

Thank you for your very kind letter. I appreciate all you say, and you worthily deserve the position you "usurp." My new theatre opens in Jany. and it was of the autumn 1900 that I wrote. I now quite understand what you demand in regard to your work & should be willing to welcome you at the St. James's under that understanding. I daresay I did not realize this before, and indeed you did not ask it of me. Please pardon me for this. I am sure we could work together should you feel willing to give it a trial. Don't bother to answer this, and sometime I hope to have a line from you saying "Yes." Give my love to the de la Rues. I have not spoken to them about this matter.

Our united regards to Mrs. Pinero and yourself. Even if we never work together again believe me I value your regard & am

Always yours sincerely

GEORGE ALEXANDER

Pinero even tried his hand at writing a libretto. The estrangement between Sullivan and Gilbert had permitted J. Comyns Carr to suggest a script for Sullivan's music. And Carr asked Pinero for assistance. The result was the failure entitled *The Beauty Stone*. It was produced at the famous Savoy Theatre, the home of the inimitable Gilbert and Sullivan comic operas.

Pinero's next experiment was in satiric comedy. *The Gay Lord Quex*, the most brilliant technical display of his genius, was performed under the leadership of John Hare at the Globe Theatre on April 8, 1898. It is too bad that this play has been forgotten,

(*He hurries away. Miss Limbird, carrying a leather bag, enters, followed by Miss Claridge and Miss Huddle.*)

Sophy. (*as she, with the aid of her girls, pins on her hat and scrambles into her coat*) You know, girls, many a silly person's head would be turned at being asked to a place like Fauncey Court — as a guest, bear in mind. But there, the houses I've been in! — it's nothing to me. Still, ~especially~ invited by ~Lady~ the Countess of Owbridge herself — (*putting her feet in turn upon a chair and hitching up her stockings*) I shall just make rather a favour of manicuring Mrs Jack. One doesn't go visiting to cut Mrs Jack's claws. Gloves! Thank ~heaven~ goodness, the evenings are long! They say it's simply heavenly at Fauncey Court — simply heaven —

(~Suddenly~ *she breaks off,* abruptly, *staring straight before her.*)

Sophy. (*under her breath*) Oh —! Fauncey Court — Lord Quex —!

Miss Claridge. (*on her R.*) What's the matter, Miss Fullgarney?

Sophy.   N—n—nothing.

Miss Moon. (*entering L.C.*) Cab, Miss Fullgarney!

Sophy. (*in an altered voice*) Bag.

(*She takes her bag from Miss Limbird and walks away, rather slowly and with her head down.*)

Sophy. (*quietly, without turning*) See you in the morning, girls.

The four girls. Good afternoon, Miss Fullgarney.

(*Sophy goes out. The curtain falls.*)

End of Act 1.

though the reason for its neglect is not hard to explain. It is a playwright's play: every idea, every social implication, every moral truth, had been sacrificed during the writing for the sake of stagecraft. Had Pinero been a musical composer seated at an organ, improvising with complete mastery of his instrument, he would have produced unorthodox harmony but revealed the resources of the instrument. The stage of the theater became his instrument in *The Gay Lord Quex;* he showed off every device known for comedy. These tricks impinge so rapidly upon one another that the result is not a play but a spectacular display.

The plot began with Sophy Fullgarney's endeavor to aid one of her customers. This simple little manicurist never existed on land or sea, but her loyalty is beautiful. There is the appeal to sentiment. All of her endeavor is to protect Muriel from disillusionment. For Muriel has announced her engagement to the gay Marquess of Quex, and Sophy has overheard Lord Quex arrange a meeting with his former mistress, the Duchess of Strood. But the plot is unimportant. What counts is the stage business; what the characters do; how they use doors and windows and keys. Pinero's stage directions are elaborate; he had thought out every movement of the actors and recorded precisely when and how the character should develop the pantomime in a particular scene. The third act develops the situation to a high point of intensity; the timing is superb; the suspense maintained until every emotional response that can be obtained has been given by the audience. But this play is entirely a matter of theatrical production. It has no meaning.

The audiences thronged to see this ingenious comedy, and the critics recognized its craftsmanship. But that is all. It had been written in competition with Oscar Wilde's scintillating comedies, *Lady Windermere's Fan*, *A Woman of No Importance*, *The Importance of Being Earnest*, which had brightly danced across the London stage. Pinero lacked Wilde's wit, the graceful phrase, and quick play upon words. Wilde easily cast the moral implications in his plays to the winds. Dexterity in plot was, however, not sufficient for competition in writing comedy. Pinero had met his master.

VII

THE MASTER-CRAFTSMAN

THE success of *The Gay Lord Quex* brought an end to Pinero's third period of experimentation and restored his confidence. For Pinero seemed to live in continual fear that he would lose his public; more than any other author of his time he sought praise for his work. Probably this craving resulted from his refusal to enter normally into the social life of the day. He took his work much too seriously for his own good. His point of view was myopic, focused on his most recent manuscript.

So the success of *The Gay Lord Quex* was good for him as a person. He felt free to travel, to relax from the frantic struggle to live up to the high reputation that *The Second Mrs. Tanqueray* had earned for him, and for a few weeks to cease looking for something new with which to win the public's favor. During this summer of 1899 he returned to Maloja and spent the month of September in the Italian lake district. While at Lake Como he became interested again in re-working the old theme of the luxury-loving woman in conflict with social and moral taboos; here in the playground of the wealthy he could treat the portrait of Paula from a new angle. So he began writing character sketches and thinking out the conflicts which he might develop. He spent the winter on the Riviera. In the spring he sailed from Marseilles on a P and O ship for England.

Pinero always traveled on the P and O line because of his friendship with Sir Thomas Sutherland. And whenever a new P and O ship was fitted out, Pinero was invariably the guest of Sir Thomas during the trial run. Pinero recalled these trips as the most delightful experiences of his life. He spent the next year and a half in travel. Finally he returned to Monte Carlo for the season of 1901 and spent April in Paris. This was the longest period that he had ever spent away from work, but he returned to England with material for several new plays.

Early in September of 1901 *The Second Mrs. Tanqueray* was revived at the Royalty Theatre. Mrs. Pat Campbell again played Paula; but this time George Arliss played Cayley Drummle and Gerald du Maurier played Captain Hugh Ardale. Both of these young men, who were to become very distinguished actors, were established in popular favor during this very successful revival.

A few weeks later, on the twenty-first, Pinero's new play, *Iris*, was performed at the Garrick Theatre. Fay Davis played the title role; Dion Boucicault, who was one of Pinero's most intimate friends, played Crocker Harrington.

Pinero changed the formula for *Iris* only slightly from that used in *The Second Mrs. Tanqueray*. Iris was the luxury-loving woman, but her past was respectable inasmuch as she had married, though not for love but for a fortune. When the play begins she is a young, attractive widow in love with a young man who cannot earn enough to support her and surround her with luxuries. The conflict arises from the fact that the will of her deceased husband had established an annuity which will stop whenever she remarries. So Iris wishes to keep young Trenwith as her lover without marrying him. Trenwith objects. This situation is further complicated by Maldonado, an international banker. He is determined to possess Iris.

When her fortune is stolen, she accepts money from Maldonado and falls into his power. Trenwith is away in Australia, trying to make his fortune. Maldonado demands that Iris become his mistress, and she complies. Thus when Trenwith comes home to marry Iris, he discovers the situation. Iris' love of luxury had destroyed her chance for happiness.

Iris is, then, a pitiably weak character. In contrast, Paula is strong. Nor has the substitution of Maldonada, merely a villain, for the part played by society in *The Second Mrs. Tanqueray* the same force. In *Iris* the conflict is between a weak woman and a villain. In *The Second Mrs. Tanqueray* the conflict is between a

~~you take Fanny Sylvain~~ in to dinner?

Kane.   Charmed. Who are your guests?

Iris.   Fanny ~~and a little~~ niece of hers whom she has ~~got~~ <u>taken under her wing,</u> dear
Croker, the Wynnings—

Kane.   Delightful.

Iris.   (*walking away from him to avoid the embarrassment of meeting his eye*) and
Mr. Trenwith. ~~(faintly)~~ (*indifferently*) Oh, and Frederick Maldonado.

Kane.   Maldonado!

Iris.   Yes.

Kane.   May I say I'm glad? The wound is healed, then?

Iris.   He writes begging me to include him again in my dinner-parties. Poor
Maldo!

        ~~(From a drawer in the writing)~~ (*She is standing beside the writing-table.
        From a drawer she takes out a ring-case and* ~~produces~~ *a tiny ring.*)

Kane.   What's that?

Iris.   (*slipping the ring on to her finger and displaying it*) A token. He gave it to
me when he — at the time — telling me that, if ever I relented, I had only to
return it to him without a word and, no matter what part of the ^{globe} ~~world~~ it
found him in, he would come to me on wings.

Kane.   The plumage is golden, in his case, Iris.

Iris.   Yes. (*closing her eyes for a moment*) But I couldn't, Archie. (*removing
the ring from her finger thoughtfully*) Yet I've been on the point of sending
this to him more than once during the past month.

Kane.   You have?

Iris.   (*mechanically,* ~~returning~~ *replacing the ring in its drawer*) As a way out of my
perplexity.

        (*The double-doors are thrown open and a servant announces "Miss* strong woman and society's refusal to forgive her past; Paula represents more than her personal problem; she is actually a symbol of a part of society against which society itself turns.

Pinero tried in every way possible to win sympathy for Iris; the problem develops from her point of view. Unfortunately, however, she remains weak and fails to discover the truth about herself until it is too late for her to make a decision. And that decision is the chief means by which a dramatist can win his audience to sympathize with a character. In that moment of decision, when the character chooses the difficult but idealistic way of life rather than the easy way, the audience responds with admiration. In the beginning of *The Second Mrs. Tanqueray*, Paula makes the decision which redeems her, which atones fully for her past, and consequently captures the audience's sympathy.

The critics in their reviews of the opening night were all mindful of *The Gay Lord Quex;* they pointed out that, in *Iris*, Pinero had faced the issues and written an honest though unpleasant denouement. But it was a matter of horror rather than pity, revulsion of the emotions rather than catharsis through awe and admiration.

Two years elapsed before Pinero presented another new play. During this period he wrote an essay on Stevenson as a dramatist in which he explained the difference between dramatic talent and theatrical talent, the point which he reiterated in analyzing Browning's plays.

At this time both Barrie and Shaw were becoming popular not merely as playwrights but as men of letters. Pinero knew that he could not compete with them and with others like them, but he wanted very much to be recognized as a dramatic author, to convince everyone that writing for the theater was distinctly different from writing for readers. This became for him an obsession at just this time. And he seemed more approachable, more willing to form new acquaintances outside the theater. But he also maintained the old associates. He wrote letters to them and sent them gifts. The following letter is not only illustrative of this attitude but significant of the reaction of his friends, who were taken by surprise.

75, Upper Berkeley Street
Portman Square. W.
Feb 4 1902

My dear Pinero

I am quite at a loss how to thank you for your beautiful present to me—Indeed I will not attempt to do so. You know what I feel about it—Your inscription has touched me more than I can express—To think that "my sympathy & encouragement" could have been of any value to you makes me feel very happy & proud—

I can only say that watching the development of your genius has ever been to me a source of the keenest pleasure & I can truly say that I have rejoiced in your successes as if they had been my own—Happy man! You are still in the prime of your manhood & many years of brilliant work still lie before you.

In the future as in the past my sympathy & heartiest best wishes will be ever with you—We have been much concerned to learn that your wife has had a sad trouble to face & also has been again very unwell—We have been away so much that we only heard of these things a few days ago—I hope that Mrs. Pinero is now more herself again, please convey to her our kindest regards—

I suppose someday or other we shall meet again. I wonder when?
Ever dear Pinero

Sincerely and gratefully yrs.

John Hare

Such a letter reveals a vast amount of understatement and omission. John Hare as actor and actor-manager had shared with Pinero many trials and surprises in the theater. Yet Pinero had drifted away from maintaining the friendships most loyal to him. No wonder his friends could not understand him.

The importance of Pinero's essay on Robert Louis Stevenson appears in the following letters from Theodore Watts-Dunton, the author of *Aylwin*, better known perhaps for his care of the celebrated poet Algernon Charles Swinburne.

The Pines
11, Putney Hill, S.W.
27 Feb. 1903

My dear Mr. Pinero,

I particularly want to see a full report of your lecture on the Drama in Scotland. I do not see a full report in *The Times*, *The Chronicle*, or *The Daily News*, but I have read comments upon it in *The Times Supplement*, & also in *The James Gazette*. Will you kindly tell me whether it has been fully reported anywhere, & also whether you are likely to publish it in pamphlet form? I was much struck with what you said about Stevenson. It is a long, long time since you promised to come to dine with us—I wonder whether it will ever come off. With kindest remembrances to Mrs. Pinero

Believe me to be,
Yours ever

THEODORE WATTS-DUNTON

THE PINES
11, PUTNEY HILL, S.W.
19th March 1903

MY DEAR MR. PINERO,

I have been exceedingly unwell or I should not have so long delayed thanking you for the charming lecture you sent me. I have read & reread it, & think it admirable. I agree with every word of it, except that I think that your praise of the mere literary qualities of Stevenson's plays excessive. But Stevenson I believe, is not so answerable for the importance of undramatic matter as his collaborateur Mr. Henley. The latter gentleman, although a very clever & even brilliant journalist, is absolutely without imagination, as his verses show, and it was a misfortune for R. L. S. that he lost so much time in collaborating with him. Your generalization about the changes in dramatic methods must be the best thing that has been written upon the subject in my time.

Don't forget your promise to come & see us. Meantime,

Believe me to be,
Yours very sincerely,

THEODORE WATTS-DUNTON

P.S. I am sure you will pardon my writing to dictation, but since I had inflamation of the eyes brought on by influenza I dictate everything.

Letty was produced at the Duke of York's Theatre on October 8, 1903. In it Pinero resumed consideration of his favorite theme: the conflict between the middle class and the aristocracy, as in *Trelawny of the "Wells."* Letty is a shop girl, flattered by the attention of Neville Letchmere. When Bernard Mandeville, her employer, proposes marriage, she tells Letchmere, hoping to arouse his jealousy and win him. But Letchmere explains that he has a wife and urges her to accept Mandeville. She is so astonished by this revelation that she accepts Mandeville.

But Mandeville proves to be rather crude at the party given by him to announce their engagement. And when Letchmere appears, Letty goes away with him to his flat. There they plan to travel together and defy the censure of society. At this juncture Letchmere receives word from his sister that she is leaving her husband to go away with her lover. This announcement permits Letty to realize her own position, and she leaves.

The last act takes place two years later. Letty has married a man of her own class and found happiness. She meets Letchmere and tells him that the finest experience of life is her simple domesticity.

William Archer was particularly pleased that, after years of pleading, Pinero had finally created a heroine motivated entirely by ideals. The failure to add to the drama of ideas disturbed Walkley, however; he felt that Pinero had reverted to his earlier story formula. And that was precisely what Pinero had done; he had told a story about stock types. For though Letty is carefully delineated, she lacks the characteristics which an author thoroughly in sympathy with the middle class could easily have portrayed. Letty never becomes more than a sentimental shopgirl who hopes to be Cinderella. Had Pinero understood her and cared to make her the symbol of her class, this play might have become a significant protest against the false order.

The remainder of the characters were merely sketched in broadest strokes, while the playwright devised ingenious situations for them, in which to come in conflict for theatrical effects.

Pinero's diffidence, his reluctance to be sociable even with such important people as W. S. Gilbert of the ever popular Gilbert and Sullivan comic operas, comes to mind as one reads the following letter.

GRIM'S DYKE, HARROW WEALD
13 June 1904

MY DEAR PINERO,

Some Tuesday in July Bourchier is going to give a benefit performance on behalf of the Bushey Heath Cottage Hospital of which I am the Hon. "Sec." His intention is to play "The Fairy's Dilemma" together with my little one-act skit on *Hamlet*, "Rosencrantz & Guildenstern" *to be played entirely by dramatic authors*, & we are anxious to know whether you will honour us by playing Rosencrantz. We played the little piece at Stanmore 18 months ago on behalf of the hospital & (with other attractions) realized £630 in two days. On that occasion Marshall played Hamlet & I played the King & unless you would like to play the King (not as good a part as Rosencrantz) we propose to cast these two parts as they were cast on that occasion. We propose to ask Burnand, H. A. Jones, and Barrie to play parts. Leo Trevor has already agreed to play the "Player." We are approaching Mrs. Craigie for the Queen & Mrs. Lacette Riley for Ophelia. What do you say? I need not tell you how highly we shall value your assistance or what an attraction your presence in the bill would be.

We had an extremely pleasant afternoon at your flat last week—but you were much missed.

Very truly yours
W. S. GILBERT

The following year, on October 9, 1904, brought a satirical comedy, *A Wife without a Smile*, to Wyndham's Theatre. Everyone was disturbed by the new play. It was stuff for the censor! Not only were the playgoers shocked but they were not particularly amused. And they looked in vain for an idea in the play which might justify Pinero's bad taste.

The cynical tone of the play exaggerates its essential vulgarity, but the humor comes not so much from either characters or situation as from a theatrical device which Walkley in the *London Times* named an erotometer. It is a dancing doll suspended through the ceiling of the Rippingill's apartment and attached to the springs of the sofa in the room above. Whenever anyone sits on the sofa, the springs of course move and cause the suspended doll to dance.

This device Rippingill created in order to make his wife laugh. The turn comes while he is laughing heartily, only to discover that it is his wife upon the sofa.

This was simple farce technique. Granted that Pinero could choose to write farce, if he wanted to do so, the fact remains that an author with a fixed philosophy of life, the determination to write searchingly about the problems of society, as Shaw was doing in *Plays Pleasant and Unpleasant*, would hardly waste his ingenuity upon such a trivial incident as formed the plot of *A Wife without a Smile*. Moreover, Pinero was shocking for no purpose; Shaw's *Widowers' Houses* had an important social thesis; but the censor failed to consider that point.

For his next play, however, Pinero resumed the theme of mis-understanding between husband and wife. He dispatched the playscript to George Alexander, with whom he had not worked for several years. Here is Alexander's reply:

57, PONT STREET S.W.

I shall make no definite plans   Oct. 13
for any play until we meet.

MY DEAR PIN,

The first two acts are all I expected them to be, lifelike and interesting from beginning to end. True comedy. Hilary could not be better or different in the earlier part of the play. It would be a great comfort to be able to begin re-hearsals on the 16th of December at latest & do the play early in January. Perhaps you will be able to say "yes" to this during the next month.

Yours

ALEC

His House in Order had its première at the St. James's Theatre on February 1, 1906, and began the most successful run of any of Pinero's plays. It finally earned for him more than two hundred thousand dollars. But, more important, it was a serious attempt to depict a typical instance of the social hypocrisy of his time.

Nina, Filmer Jesson's second wife, was merely Derek's govern-ess. Neither father nor small son can forget that. This of course is the old theme of class distinctions, developed previously in *The Second Mrs. Tanqueray* and especially in *Letty*. But the new devel-opment comes from the fact that Jesson constantly compares Nina with his first wife, Annabel. Annabel's superiority is em-phasized by Jesson's dedication of a park in her memory and the coming of her family for this ceremony.

Jesson's brother, Hilary, also comes and discovers Nina's plight, but he accomplishes nothing in her defense. Hilary is Cayley Drummle from *The Second Mrs. Tanqueray* and Crocker Harring-ton from *Iris*, revitalized by a deeper philosophic attitude. (This was the part taken by Alexander.)

The turn in the plot comes when Nina discovers that Derek is not Jesson's child and that the saintly Annabel had been un-faithful. Here is her much-desired opportunity for revenge.

Then Hilary convinces her that her revelation will bring un-
happiness to all concerned. As a result Nina does not take her
revenge. But the abuse of Nina continues. At this juncture
Hilary reveals the truth to his brother and to Annabel's brother.
And amends are forthwith made to the long-suffering Nina.

The advance made in this play is not entirely in Pinero's willingness to think the problem through to the end. He has sacrificed cleverness in order to develop the characters. But the dialogue becomes heavy at times, as Hilary emphasizes the philosophic implications. Pinero had at last come upon an idea worthy
of his skill in dramaturgy.

Among Pinero's papers occurs the following bit of doggerel, the
authorship of which is uncertain, possibly better forgotten.

> His House in Order Alexander sets—
> An actor neat & manager of nous
> So now a crowded audience he gets
> Without a single order in his House.

Early in 1907 Pinero was taken ill. When he was able to travel,
he crossed from Dover to Ostend and then proceeded up the
Rhine to Weisbaden, where he spent several months.

It was at this time that William S. Gilbert was knighted by
King Edward VII, and Pinero sent his congratulations. Gilbert's
reply is reprinted here because of its prophecy to be fulfilled two
years later.

GRIM'S DYKE, HARROW WEALD
1st July 1907

MY DEAR PINERO,

I cannot thank you enough for your cordial words of congratulation. I suppose it was given to me in recognition of extreme (not to say doddering) old age.
It will be many years (happily for us all) before you will qualify for it on that
score—or rather, on that three score and ten—but it will come to you for much
pleasanter reasons. *Hodie mihi cras tibi.*

Kindest regards to Mrs. Pinero & Miss Hamilton.

Very sincerely yours
W. S. GILBERT

During the next year Pinero wrote *The Thunderbolt*. This
proved to be in many respects his most significant attempt at

writing social drama. It was performed at the St. James's Theatre on May 9, 1908.

It was not a formula play. Instead of striving for another point of view from which to write about the misunderstanding between husband and wife, he took a much broader social problem and made of it an ironic comedy.

The theme raises the question whether a daughter by a common-law marriage deserves to inherit her father's fortune. The brothers and sister of Edward Mortimore did not know of his daughter, Helen Thornhill. So when he dies they expect to divide his fortune among themselves. The younger brother, Thaddeus, has long been disregarded, however, by his other relatives because, in marrying Phyllis, they felt he had married beneath his class. But Thaddeus and Phyllis are loyal to each other; in fact, they live for their children.

Edward Mortimore had made a will, the solicitors insist, leaving his fortune to Helen Thornhill, but the will cannot be found. Consequently, the greed of the Mortimores overwhelms their sense of justice. Then Helen Thornhill appears; she is ignored by everyone except Phyllis. As a result of Helen's interest in Phyllis' children, Phyllis confesses to everyone's astonishment that she destroyed Edward Mortimore's will. This is the thunderbolt.

Though the greedy brothers and sisters have proof of Phyllis' crime, they cannot force Helen to prosecute. In fact Helen tries to forgive the only member of the Mortimore family who had been kind. On the other hand, Phyllis had acted in behalf of her children on the false reasoning that she did not know the person mentioned in the will and consequently acted for the good of the family. The fact that Helen shares the estate equally with all of the Mortimores brings the play to its end.

It is of course ironic that the brothers and sisters thus share in their brother's estate only because of the crime committed by their younger brother's wife. But the deeper ironic point lies in the friendship formed between Helen and Phyllis, for Phyllis had destroyed the will and then confessed to doing so because the unknown person had become her friend.

This play did not involve only tried and true characters. Everyone had freshness and vitality directly from Pinero's own observation and genius for creation. Furthermore, the action was more unified in time and place than ever before. Finally, the characters are provincial, dominated by petty standards and false values.

Although this type of play, without hero or heroine, has become familiar to present-day playgoers, it was distinctly an innovation in 1908. And the pervading tone of cynicism was Pinero's own. Bourgeois characters portrayed against the background of provincialism fail to solve their problems. Thus the play becomes an indictment of human greed and folly rather than the failure of an individual.

In the *London Times* Walkley excessively praised Pinero's originality, the individuality of his talent, and the directness and rapidity with which the author developed the theme. The reviewer for the *Era* stated his conviction that the play was so unconventional in its treatment of character that it was "literature." Of all the critics only Hamilton Fyfe, who was then reviewing for the *World*, found fault with the play, suggesting that the characterization was flimsy, the plot too long drawn out, though extremely clever and ingenious in particular scenes.

King Edward VII recognized Pinero's contribution to the drama by giving him a knighthood in the spring of 1909.

On September 2, 1909, *Mid-Channel* was produced at the St. James's Theatre. In New York, at the Empire Theatre on January 31, 1910, Ethel Barrymore began a successful run as Zoe in *Mid-Channel*. For the scene of his new play Pinero turned from the provincial town to London, and in particular to a fashionable drawing-room in the West End.

Superficially *Mid-Channel* resembles *The Second Mrs. Tanqueray*. In both plays the plot involves an erring wife, a misunderstanding husband, and their mutual friend, who becomes the *raisonneur*. But here the similarity ends. Zoe craves excitement, and her indiscretions become the action of the play; whereas Paula had a past, and her attempts to live for her husband are thwarted. In the end, however, both women meet their nemesis.

Zoe's husband, Theodore Blundell, motivates her revolt. He has sacrificed everything in order to make money; in middle age he is selfish and inconsiderate of Zoe's interests. On the other hand, Paula's husband, Aubrey Tanqueray, had been willing to sacrifice everything for Paula's happiness.

Peter Mottram, the mutual friend, has more to do than had Cayley Drummle, for Peter has to reconcile husband and wife and reconcile their conflicts.

The plot of *Mid-Channel* becomes more complex than that of *The Second Mrs. Tanqueray* because of Zoe's activities. She goes with young men, whom she calls her tame Robins, to the theater, to dinner, and to dance. Thus she becomes involved in the love affair of Leonard Ferris and Ethel Pierpoint. She leaves her husband and induces young Ferris to follow her to Italy. Her husband seeks solace in an affair of his own. But in the end, like Paula, Zoe realizes that she has destroyed all her expectations for happiness and commits suicide.

This ending, like that of *The Second Mrs. Tanqueray*, is motivated by what the heroine says in the opening act of the play: both declare their dependence upon their husband's love; but Zoe is more jealous than Paula. In fact, Zoe's actions within the scope of the play itself make her less the object of sympathy.

Neither Zoe nor Paula is static; the development of both characters takes place within the play. But Zoe degenerates, whereas Paula becomes idealistic. Paula's plight consequently evokes pity; Zoe's arouses horror.

The critics were not of one mind in reviewing the première. In the *Stage*, September 9, 1909, Sir George Alexander was quoted as saying that he believed *Mid-Channel* represented Pinero's most serious and memorable work. And with that opinion the reviewer concurred. In the *Era* the critic highly praised the strength of the vital characterizations and supreme technique.

In the *World* Fyfe damned the play with faint praise for its unconventionality and frankness. In the *London Times* the reviewer found the play unpleasant, the characters brutal, the slang impossible. But his criticism lacked the fundamental understanding of dramatic motives to which Mr. Walkley had for many years accustomed the readers of that distinguished newspaper.

Pinero had, however, reached the zenith of his career. The younger critics were predisposed to find him old fashioned because of his continuance of the triangle, his absorption with the double standard. Certainly his themes were becoming repetitious and he had little new to say; but his skill was increasing, and he presented very deftly highly complex groupings of character for the delight of the theater audience.

VIII

ANTICLIMAX

THE year 1910 marked the turning-point in Pinero's career. He was fifty-five. He had written more than thirty successful plays. He had achieved a secure position far beyond his youthful goal. And yet the plays which he was to write during the next twenty years were not to add to but to detract from his reputation. He had lost his point of view.

A dramatist for the commercial theater must know the interests of the people. His search for material is like the news reporter's; both must recognize the fundamental cross-currents of society. As a young man, Pinero had been keen to detect the main movements of thought. But as he grew older his absorption with stagecraft apparently blotted out his knowledge of people and the ideas by which men live.

His security made him reactionary. He wanted the world to remain as he had known it when he won his first struggles toward recognition. But the society of 1910 was no longer complacent. A world-revolution was fomenting; the proletariat clamored for a spokesman. Bernard Shaw was preaching the social gospel, but in terms understandable only to the intellectuals and liberals among the bourgeoisie. And Shaw was making progress, rapidly attaining a unique position among the English playwrights because of his ideas. Galsworthy realized what was taking place, and from his restricted point of view as a man of property he exhibited remarkable tolerance and liberality.

The onrush of the cataclysmic events leading to the World War did not excite Pinero. His new acquaintances were not of the people. He was the entertainer par excellence of the privileged class; he had the rich man's philosophy, the desire to preserve what he had gained, regardless of social trends.

No wonder the generation of critics coming to the theater in 1910 found Pinero old fashioned. In comparison with the younger writers he was hopelessly inarticulate. He still possessed his wizardry in handling material for the stage, but he had nothing whatsoever to say in *Preserving Mr. Panmure*, produced at the Comedy Theatre on January 19, 1911.

When George Alexander, the actor-manager who had shared the profits of Pinero's greatest successes, was knighted, Pinero sent his congratulations. Alexander's reply is more interesting.

> 57, PONT STREET, S.W.
> 26 June 1911

MY DEAR PIN.

Your letter is dated 21st June. I ought to have answered it sooner. I have written to many friends, but I find it difficult to say, what my heart dictates, to you. I am deeply sensible of how much gratitude I owe to your "written words." You have enabled me to win distinction & money too, and these two things mean a lot in our short lives. That my good luck is pleasant to you is a *delight* to me & my wife

> Yours aff-ly
>
> GEORGE ALEXANDER

This letter shows how far apart Pinero and Alexander really were as persons, despite the mutual assistance they had experienced. Pinero had become increasingly aloof, a little superior to his old friends in the theater. And yet at this time he was writing a play about theatrical people, nothing new, but a restatement of the old theme used in *Trelawny of the "Wells."* In the extremely class-conscious society of the day Pinero felt very sharply his connection with the theater; he was sensitive, despite his honors; he questioned even now, as he had in his younger days, the place of the theatrical people in society. But his point of view had changed with his financial position. In *Trelawny of the "Wells"* he was still one of the profession. As he wrote the dialogue for *The "Mind the Paint" Girl* his attitude was rather like that of an elderly and distinguished barrister recollecting adventures of his hot-blooded youth.

On Saturday, February 17th, 1912, at 7.45 o'clock,

and on subsequent Evenings at 8.30,

MR. CHARLES FROHMAN

PRESENTS

THE "MIND THE PAINT" GIRL.

A COMEDY IN FOUR ACTS

BY

ARTHUR PINERO.

On Saturday, February 17th, 1912, at 7.45, and on subsequent Evenings at 8.30,

MR. CHARLES FROHMAN

PRESENTS

THE "MIND THE PAINT" GIRL.

A Comedy, in Four Acts, by

ARTHUR PINERO.

THE PERSONS OF THE PLAY.

Viscount Farncombe	Mr. VERNON STEEL
Colonel the Hon. Arthur Stidulph ...	Mr. CHARLES DORAN
Baron Von Rettenmayer	Mr. LOUIS GOODRICH
Captain Nicholas Jeyes...	Mr. ALLAN AYNESWORTH
Lionel Roper	Mr. DION BOUCICAULT
Sam de Castro	Mr. NIGEL PLAYFAIR
Herbert Fulkerson	Mr. FRANK DENTON
Stewart Heneage	Mr. W. CADOGAN
Gerald Grimwood	Mr. E. DOUGLAS
Carlton Smythe. (Manager of the Pandora Theatre)	Mr. CHARLES E. VERNON
Douglas Glynn, Albert Palk, Wilfrid Tavish, and Sigismund Shirley } (Actors at the Pandora)	Messrs. A. FITZGERALD, WENLOCK BROWN, CECIL NEWTON & NORMAN YATES
Vincent Bland. (A Musical Composer, attached to the Pandora)	Mr. BERNARD MEREFIELD
Morris Cooling. (Business Manager at the Pandora) ...	Mr. JOHN TRESAHAR
Luigi. (Maître d'hôtel at Catani's Restaurant) ...	Mr. J. WOODALL-BIRDE
Waiters	Messrs. A. THORN, E. THIRLBY and J. MEGUS.
The Hon. Mrs. Arthur Stidulph. (Formerly, as Dolly Ensor, of the Pandora Theatre)	Miss RUTH MACKAY
Lily Parradell	Miss MARIE LÖHR
Jimmie Birch	Miss GWENDOLINE BROGDEN
Gabrielle Kato	Miss NINA SEVENING
Enid Moncrieff	Miss HILDA MOORE
Daphne Dure	Miss DORIS MACINTYRE
Nita Trevenna } (Of the Pandora)	Miss MARJORIE DORÉ
Flo Connify	Miss GEORGINA MILNE
Sybil Dermott	Miss ALMA DUDLEY
Olga Cook	Miss GWENDOLINE JESSON
Evangeline Ventris	Miss MARGARET KING
Mrs. Upjohn. (Lily Parradell's mother) ...	Miss CLARE GREET
Gladys. (Lily's parlourmaid)	Miss ZOE GORDON
Maud. (Lily's maid)	Miss GLADYS BRENDA

The action of the piece takes place in London—at LILY PARRADELL'S house in Bloomsbury, in the foyer of the Pandora Theatre, and again at LILY'S house. The curtain will be lowered for a few moments in the course of the Second Act.

A Gong will be sounded upon the stage one minute before the rising of the curtain upon each Act.

84

The Costumes worn by Miss Löhr, Miss Moore, Miss Mackay and Miss Sevening, designed and executed by LUCILE, LTD., 23, Hanover Square. The remainder of the Costumes by Madame HANDLEY-SEYMOUR, 47-48, New Bond Street.

The Scenery painted by Messrs. W. HANN & SON

Furniture by Messrs. OETZMANN.

General Manager · · · · Mr. W. LESTOCQ.

Matinees Every Thursday and Saturday at 2.30.

Business Manager · · · · Mr. JAMES W. MATHEWS.

Stage Manager · · · · Mr. DUNCAN McRAE.

Musical Director · · · · · Mr. JOHN CROOK.

PRICES OF ADMISSION—Private Boxes, £4 4s., £3 3s., and £1 11s. 6d.; Orchestra Stalls, 10s. 6d.; Balcony Stalls, 7s. 6d.; Dress Circle, 6s.; Upper Circle, 4s.; Pit, 2s. 6d.; Gallery, 1s.

Box Office 10 to 10. Telephones, GERRARD, 312, 313, 314.

MIND THE PAINT (the complete song), words by D'Arcy Wingate, music by Vincent Bland, as originally sung by MISS LILY PARRADELL at the Pandora Theatre in the Musical Play of " THE DUCHESS OF BRIXTON," may be obtained from Messrs. Church and Co. (Ltd.), Music Publishers, 181, New Bond Street.

AFTER THE THEATRE. CATANI'S RESTAURANT, 459, Strand. Best *cuisine* in London. Milanese band. Private rooms. Urbano Catani, Sole Proprietor. Tel: 10,337, Gerrard.

G. HARMSWORTH & Co., Printers, &c., 148, Drury Lane, London.

85

Extract from the Rules made by the Lord Chamberlain.

(1) The name of the actual and responsible Manager of the Theatre must be printed on every play bill.

(2) The Public can leave the Theatre at the end of the performance by all exit and entrance doors, which must open outwards.

(3) Where there is a Fire-proof screen to the proscenium opening, it must be lowered at least once during every performance to ensures it being in proper working order.

(4) Smoking is not permitted in the Auditorium.

(5) All gangways, passages and staircases must be kept free from chairs or any other obstructions, whether permanent or temporary.

In the closing months of his life Pinero referred to this play as his best. He disagreed with my opinion that the play was distinctly artificial in its presentation of theatrical life. For example, Lily Parradell, the heroine, is one of the Pandora Girls. She is not only the toast of the gay blades but is offered marriage by young Viscount Francombe. She is in love with Francombe but feels her obligation to Captain Jeyes, who has given her the chance for success. Her intimacy with Jeyes, whom she calls "Nicko," is represented as platonic. But he is jealous of her and tries to frustrate her romance with Francombe.

"Certainly Lily was the exception!" I objected, defending my opinion of the play.

"She redeemed them all!" declared Sir Arthur, without the slightest hesitation.

Obviously, Pinero was idealizing his heroine, as he had every right to do. But in so doing he was earning for himself the criticism which I had been reading in the reviews of the première; namely, that he lacked a fixed ethical point of view.

Though Francombe wins Lily in the end and Nicko is revealed a weakling, nobody cares. The complications were resolved readily because they never really existed. Lily's deep loyalty to Nicko was not based upon affection; she might even be regarded as having paid in full for his assistance by her success. But Pinero was concerned with blessing the marriage between a member of the nobility and an actress. Lily's future in society must be secure at all costs. In *Trelawny of the "Wells"* Rose discovered that an actress can find happiness only in her work.

Times were changing. Society was accepting theatrical people as it had not in Pinero's youth. In 1912 this situation in the light of world-events seemed trivial—of little real importance to people about to fight for democracy.

The following letter from Lord Esher reveals, however, the reaction of the special audience for which Pinero's plays were still valid. The importance of this letter can therefore scarcely be overstated. It reveals, furthermore, what has been previously deduced from the play itself: that Pinero had become reactionary.

2, Tilney Street, Mayfair, W.
28 Feb. 1912

Duke of York's Theatre

My dear Sir Arthur,

What extraordinary creatures 'critics' are!

I don't suppose any play ever written here or in Norway, can be said to be more skillful or to touch more truthfully or with a more certain hand, those particular chords in human nature which you set out to make vibrate.

It really is marvellous that while about every branch of art and literature has risen to a higher average level in recent times, criticism should have remained as dull and undiscerning as it was in the XVIIIth century.

We thought the play wonderful. Faultless, if I may say so, if judged by the simple test of whether you have succeeded in doing what you meant to do.

I hope you won't think this an impertinence, but I have not enjoyed an evening more for years, although I feel worn out!

Yours always sincerely,

Esher

For Lord Esher the play was right. And Pinero had lost none of his skill in stagecraft. In illustration of his ability to organize material for the stage consider the second act, located in the refreshment saloon of the theater. The time is immediately after the evening performance. The occasion is a birthday party for Lily.

Into this room come the company and their friends. The problem is to maintain the continuity of thought and action throughout the group. And Pinero, as if writing for his own pleasure in displaying his mastery of technique, introduces one group or couple after another, their dialogue impinging so closely on what has been said that the audience or reader senses no distortion of the scene; the illusion of actual life is always supreme.

Indisputably he lavishes his greatest care on the dialogue. For he had been angered by the critics' attacks on his attempts to use colloquial speech in *Mid-Channel*. From the precise articulation of Viscount Farncombe to the various dialectal inflections of Sam de Castro, Baron von Rettenmayor, and Hugh Fulkerson, the language is not only valid but characterizing.

It must be remembered, however, that in 1912 Shaw wrote *Pygmalion*, sweeping aside all competition for honors in writing

London dialects. And though Pinero wrote his best dialogue, it was not good enough; he was hopelessly outclassed.

In America, however, Pinero was enjoying a vogue, chiefly because Daniel Frohman was producing with rare understanding of stagecraft the plays Pinero had written during the previous decade.

At this time Henry Arthur Jones was in America to receive an honorary Master of Arts degree from Harvard University. The following letter indicates Jones's unselfish and warm regard for his long-standing rival.

HOTEL MARIE ANTOINETTE
BROADWAY 66TH TO 67TH STREET, NEW YORK
April 1st 1912

MY DEAR PINERO,

It has been announced that you are coming over to America next autumn. The American dramatists want to give you a dinner, and from my experience of their hospitality, it will be a good and hearty one. Charles Klein, their secretary and the chairman of their committee, has asked me to convey their invitation to you. He is known to you as a successful dramatist; he will then be known to you, as he has long been known to me, as a jolly good fellow. You will meet with unbounded good fellowship and kindness and appreciation on this side—

I have had a very splendid time over here, spite of an unlucky play that contained a court scene after three plays had just been doing one—I have stayed over here for the Spring, as England and coal strikes and the March climate were not seductive.

I expect to be back about the end of May. Please give my warm salutations to our friends at the next lunch of the Dramatists' Club

Always faithfully yrs,

HENRY ARTHUR JONES

Will you send a line of reply to

CHARLES KLEIN
ROWAYTON
CONN. U.S.A.

Pinero's next two plays merit no comment. *The Widow of Wasdale Head*, a fantasy, was produced at the Duke of York's Theatre on October 14, 1912; and *Playgoers*, a Domestic Episode, was produced at the St. James's Theatre on March 31, 1913.

After an interval of two years, Pinero appeared with a new

play, *The Big Drum*. This was produced at the St. James's Theatre on September 1, 1915, and was given one hundred performances. Into this play Pinero poured forth all of his pent-up emo-
tion about aggressive literary men—self-advertisers. In fact Pinero felt so strongly about the matter that the play suffers from
overemphasis in satire.

Philip Mackworth, an unsuccessful young novelist, wants to
marry Ottoline Filson. But her parents, social climbers, oppose
the marriage because of his failure to make money. He consequently writes a commercially successful novel. Ottoline's brother discovers, however, that the twenty-five thousand copies
were not sold to the public but to his sister. Hence Pinero con-
cludes that a great many writers lack modesty. Obviously the
thought is confused. The playwright allows his resentment
against certain well-known contemporaries to run away with his
argument. He finds publicity of any kind much to be deplored.
But in this attitude, whether he was right or not, he was reactionary. The age of advertising had come; publicity stunts were the
vogue; the public could hardly be expected to regard his old-
school reticence with interest.

Had Pinero granted interviews, expressed his opinions on any
subject with charm and facetiousness, visited influential drawing-
rooms, shot big game in India, his own reputation would not
have plummeted so rapidly. His simple failure to be a good fellow, to be more than a playwright, defeated his becoming a public figure long after his plays were no longer important. Bernard
Shaw observed many of these necessary amenities rather well!

As a result of writing a discerning essay on Robert Louis Stevenson as a dramatist, Pinero became acquainted with Mrs. Stevenson. The following letter indicates her appreciation and interest in his work.

Stonehedge
R.D. Route No. 1
Santa Barbara

Dear Mr. Pinero,

The advent of your play has filled my whole family, as well as myself, with
joy and gratitude, also despair. The latter because "thanks awfully" seems such

an inadequate return for so much. If I could but send you some bottled climate, or offer Mrs. Pinero one of my orange trees in full bloom or heavy with fruit— they do both at the same time—! But alas and alas.

I think I told you of my project of trying a haunted house? Well, not only has the purchase been made, but I have rebuilt the hideous old house, turning it into an Italian villa of sorts. It was great fun in the doing, as I made it all myself with the aid of an intelligent carpenter in defiance of the architects. Puffed up with pride, I send you in this some snapshots, made by the intelligent carpenter, showing a view of the back premises and one corner of the front verandah. Many beautiful, large trees prevent our getting any other views. I should like to send fifty.

The ghost we have not, as yet, seen, though we have offered her every opportunity for an effective and dramatic appearance.

I think if you realize what a charming place Santa Barbara is, and how warm your welcome at Stonehedge, you would ask Mrs. Pinero to get ready her "steamer trunk," and in a fortnight's time we should be meeting you at the little Santa Barbara station. This is a good place to rest in and a good place to play. Come and play with us, and incidentally rest. I have birds, and trees, and flowers, and sea, and many different kinds of sport to offer you—oh I have many things to offer both you and Mrs. Pinero would love!

Lloyd and Ned Field send many friendly messages to you both—and here I am at the end of this note with only a commonplace "thanks awfully" after all. Please put into it all the things I mean, and with warm regards to Mrs. Pinero, believe me,

Yours most sincerely,

FANNY STEVENSON

Another interval of insignificant work followed. These plays are enumerated for the sake of the record: *Mr. Livermore's Dream: A Lesson in Thrift*, was produced at the Coliseum on January 15, 1916. *The Freaks: An Idyll of Suburbia*, was produced at the New Theatre on February 14, 1918; and also in 1918 came *Monica's Blue Boy*, a play without words to the music of Sir Frederick Cowen.

Lady Pinero died in 1919, after a long illness. For a man of Pinero's temperament this experience was particularly difficult. He had long depended upon his wife to keep his little world in order; the maintenance of his strictly observed routine. All arrangement of his social life now became his problem, for she had tried to maintain for him the friendships he found so little time to cultivate. But now many of his older friends were dead, and the new ones were not easy for him to hold. He was a pitiably lonely man.

Mrs. Claude Neville Hughes came regularly to his house to spend with him the usual morning hours, for years devoted to relaxation. After her mother's death Mrs. Hughes tried to help him fill in those hours for which he was so dependent upon his wife's company and calls of friends. Sometimes they talked; more often he sat in his favorite chair by the fireside and dozed, indicating his happiness that she was with him by smiling and then, as if realizing that she must be bored, suggesting a drive through nearby Regent's Park or through the Oxford shopping district.

Pinero was particularly lonely because he had never permitted a telephone to be installed in his house. A letter by special messenger was his favorite form of communication, even for trivial matters. Here is an example.

> 115 A HARLEY STREET W. 1.
> Monday Morning.
>
> DEAREST TINA,
>
> Of course I will dine with you and Hughes, and show you my suspenders again, on Thursday. Delighted. I am getting to be asked out a great deal through wearing suspenders. What a little makes one popular in these days! See you tomorrow, I hope.
>
> Yours
>
> EBE

This letter to Lady Pinero's daughter, addressed with the pet name he gave her and signed with her name for him, indicates the depth of his disillusionment and bitterness about the new order. The cynicism suffusing all of his work had point in his younger years, gave tone to his plays. But it made him a pitiable object of despair as an old man.

Months went by after the death of Lady Pinero without his attempting to write a line of dialogue.

Then came *Quick Work*, a story of war marriage. It was produced in America, at the Court Square Theatre, Springfield, Massachusetts, on November 17, 1919, without success. It was merely a bit of fluff. For Pinero had no grasp of what the war actually meant to the young. The clever manipulation of puppet-like characters and stagecraft developed without an idea, when other playwrights were explaining what the war meant to vital characters.

On February 21, 1922, *A Seat in the Park* was produced at the Winter Garden Theatre. This play, too, lacked important characters.

On March 1, of the same year, *The Enchanted Cottage*, produced at the Duke of York's Theatre, offered much more substance than any other plays in this final period of his career. And twelve years later, a few weeks before he died, *The Enchanted Cottage* was produced by Royal Command of Their Majesties during their holiday in Edinburgh. But even this remembrance scarcely mitigated the gloom which had settled on him in the days of his lost prestige.

The weakness of *The Enchanted Cottage* is to be found in the peculiar mixture of cynicism and sentiment. It is the kind of material which Sir James Barrie delineated best—a fantasy of sentiment pregnant with delicate implications. But Pinero could not shake off his own bitterness. He himself described it as a fable; Barrie would have made it seem true; he would have created the illusion of reality in this brief escape from the cruelty of reality.

In *The Enchanted Cottage* a wounded war veteran named Bashford seeks escape from the solicitude of his relatives. Living near his cottage is an unattractive woman whom he asks to marry him. Major Hillgrove, another neighbor, who lost his sight in the war, believes that marriage has transformed both Bashford and Laura, brought him strength and her beauty, because of what Mrs. Minnett, their old servant, tells him. They too believe that something has transformed them and in a dream they live as Mrs. Minnett described them to Major Hillgrove. But on the following day Bashford's relatives arrive and can find no trace of the transformation about which Major Hillgrove has told them. And so both Bashford and Laura become disillusioned; nevertheless, they feel that they have found happiness.

The dream structure of the second episode gave Pinero opportunity for resuming brilliantly his old mastery over stagecraft. The deception of the blind man and the intent of the servant are, however, weaknesses in the development of the idea. For Pinero had to disillusion his sentimental couple, if only to reveal his own mood. This conflict between cynicism and sentiment thus distorts the point of the play: a disenchanted cottage hardly preserves the happiness of its dwellers. And why did Mrs. Minnett deceive them if only to add mental suffering to the war veteran's physical pain? It is as if to assert that the mind can make a heaven of hell and then declare that there is no mind!

Some months in advance of the dinner given at the Garrick Club in honor of Sir Arthur, on Sunday, February 12, 1928, Sir Anthony Hope Hawkins wrote the following letter:

> 13th Oct: 27
> HEATH FARM
> WALTON-ON-THE-HILL
> TADWORTH, SURREY.

MY DEAR SIR ARTHUR,

I feel myself very highly honoured by being chosen to be the mouthpiece of the Garrick Club at the dinner in your honour. Whatever may be the imperfections in what I say, you may at least feel sure that it will be the tribute of a very sincere admirer, and that I shall have taken pains to make it be some measure worthy of its subject.

> Yours very truly
> ANTHONY H. HAWKINS

Pinero's speech on that occasion I have before me, seven and a half typewritten, quarto-size pages. At the top he has written: "My speech at the Dinner given to me at the Garrick Club on Sunday, February 17th, 1928."

MY DEAR HAWKINS—MY DEAR FRIENDS—

Thank you. I thank you all from the bottom of my heart, You are too good to me. Thank you.

And there I should like to leave off and to be allowed to sit down again; but of course I must try to make some sort of a speech in acknowledgment of the great compliment you are paying me, and anticipating the ordeal I should have to face tonight—and it has been a bit of an ordeal, I assure you, to listen to such generous overpraise as I have received from Sir Anthony Hope Hawkins— anticipating the ordeal I should have to face to-night, I have thought over a way in which I can best convey to you my deep sense of obligation. I shall not detain you at the furtherest more than two minutes, but I want to give you just an outline of a chapter in the story of my life. It is a romantic chapter. Every man's life, however insignificant it may be, is a romance to himself. The title of this chapter is "The Garrick Club."

My acquaintance with the Garrick Club began in the early 'seventies—in eighteen seventy-one or two. At that time, a long series of family misfortunes having made it necessary, young as I was, that I should go out into the world, I was employed, with one other lad, in the office of a solicitor with a limited practice in Lincoln's Inn Fields. My salary at the start was a pound a week; afterwards it was raised to twenty-five shillings, and subsequently to one-pound-ten. The last named sum represents, pecuniarily, my supreme achievement in pursuit of my father's, and my grandfather's profession—the law. I hope I earned my wage, but I confess I have grave misgivings on the point. The truth is I was stage-struck almost from childhood, and while I was in Lincoln's Inn Fields I was often guilty of suborning my companion and, behind my employer's back composing dramas and sending them about to the various theatres. My manuscripts were always accompanied by a letter written, to impress the recipient, on my employer's note-paper, and I remember how discomfited I was on one occasion when inadvertently he opened a letter from a London manager addressed to myself, saying "Dear Sir, Your stuff is of no earthly use to me. For God's sake, fetch it away as soon as possible."

Now, gentlemen, I am not going to weary you with a tale of trials and difficulties. I may tell you, however, that, notwithstanding the money I earned in Lincoln's Inn Fields, I was exceedingly poor in those early 'seventies. Most of my salary—my pound, my five-and-twenty shillings, and my one-pound-ten— went, so desperate was the need, into a common purse at home, and to find myself with half-a-crown in my pocket of my very own was an experience as exciting as it was rare. But a stage-struck youth is never wholly unhappy. To be stage-struck is to have visions, and to live largely in dream-land, and to be the most ardent of hero worshippers; and worshippers of theatrical idols have frequent opportunities of feasting their eyes on the objects of their adoration. And this is where the Garrick Club comes in. Like young Norval in the play, who "had heard of battles and longed to follow to the field some warlike lord," I had heard of the Garrick Club as a club which counted the most eminent actors among its members, and I longed to track those great men to their lair.

Now, the luncheon-hour in Lincoln's Inn Fields—dinner-hour it was then called—was from one till two; but, owing to circumstances I have hinted at, my luncheon was seldom of such volume and substance as to absorb the whole of that hour of freedom. So it was my custom, as soon as I had swallowed my meal, to dart off to Garrick Street, to station myself opposite the club, and to watch these windows in the confident expectation of catching sight of some prominent actor enjoying a more substantial repast than that of which I had just partaken. In this way I first beheld in their private characters a young John Hare and a young S. B. Bancroft, who in a later year were to be my proposer and seconder for membership of the club. I must have seen also many others of renown, though I dare say in my eagerness I often mistook a learned judge or barrister for a popular comedian.

Well, in the summer of 1874, the fortunes of my belongings having somewhat improved, I threw up my berth in Lincoln's Inn Fields and, as the saying goes, went upon the stage. I obtained an engagement at the Theatre Royal, Edinburgh, to play what was known in theatrical parlance as General Utility—a line of business which involved my appearing as the Swell, with Dundreary whiskers, in the "comic scenes" of the pantomime. I recollect, without gratification, that I was heavily lathered by the clown and shaved with a wooden razor. In 1876 I was in London again—a London actor. In 1881 I had done with acting and had become a dramatic author, and it was as a dramatic author that in 1887 I was elected to membership of the Garrick Club. In 1899 I was regarded as a person of sufficient mental and moral responsibility to be entitled to sit on the General Committee and, with the usual intervals, I have continued to do so ever since. But I can no longer count upon those refreshing intervals, for two years ago I was chosen to be one of your three Trustees. And to-day, when I am eating my lunch at this window—my favorite seat—I look out into Garrick Street and in my mind's eye I see a shabbily dressed youth with hardly a penny to bless himself with, and with very doubtful prospects, standing on the other side of the street gazing wistfully in this direction; and I can scarcely believe that I was once that youth, and that the visions he saw and the dreams he dreamt have more or less materialized—one of the most glorious of those visions, one of the most fantastic of those dreams, being that someday he would have the right to enter the portals of the Garrick Club.

There, gentlemen, you have, more fully than I intended to narrate it, my chapter of romance. Forgive me for exceeding my two minutes; my desire to enable you to perceive how much this gathering means to me—how it adds a blaze of spendour to my romantic chapter—has made me break my promise to speak only a few words. I will say no more—except this: that if I had as many years before me as I have left behind me, there would not be a single day on which I would not recall with pride and gratitude the honour you have done me to-night.

This speech to the members of the Garrick Club constitutes Pinero's autobiography; three essays, "Robert Louis Stevenson: The Dramatist," "Browning as a Dramatist," and "The Drama of the 'Seventies," together with the Foreword to *Two Plays*, express his theories about his craft. The speech is, however, notable for the deep strain of sentiment, if not sentimentality, with which the elderly dramatist in his period of disillusionment seldom spoke. The strictly maintained objectivity of his plays revealed only cynicism based upon his philosophy of fatalism.

On May 14, 1928, *A Private Room* was produced at the Little Theatre without much success; but the production was not without admirers. Lord Mersey's letter reveals that the older generation had not forgotten him.

22, GROSVENOR PLACE, S.W.
23 Sept. 1928

MY DEAR A. W. PINERO

Accept my warm thanks for the pamphlet you have so kindly sent to me. I have read it word for word with great interest and I now appreciate the difficulty of the task which you have imposed on yourself.

Eighty years ago I used to buy (as far as my coppers would go) Skelt's *Miller and His Men* and other blood curdling dramas. I bought them plain and my hand from a very cheap paint box applied the colours. What joy it was! and how willingly the household attended the first performance.

God bless you: our tastes in our early days were much the same and our memories are now on the same times.

Always yours,
MERSEY

In 1930 Pinero published *Two Plays*, with a Foreword; one of them, "Dr. Harmer's Holidays," was performed without success at the Schubert-Belasco Theatre, Washington, D.C., on March 16, 1931. Its theme of hypocrisy was treated with intense bitterness: Dr. Harmer's double life merely lacked interest because he was utterly worthless. The other play, "Child Man," pointed out that an author with a reputation for portrayal of childhood despised children. He enjoyed writing historical studies which he could not give away but acceded to his wife's demands to interpret childhood and in so doing acquired fame and fortune. So biting was Pinero's attack in both these plays that he seemed to have no other purpose than to denounce the stupidity of mankind; but if humanity has no redeeming qualities whatsoever, why bother?

Pinero's last play to be produced was entitled *A Cold June;* its première was at the Duchess Theatre on May 20, 1932.

The personal disappointments brought failure to his work for the theater in this last period of his career. He had been unable to keep abreast of the times, to understand the new order, and to compete with the younger writers. He himself was old fashioned before ever he set pen to manuscript. He lacked a philosophy sufficient to accept the situation. So, unfortunately, he continued to write more or less as he had before the war, but bitterly, as if he knew he had already burned out the genius which had sustained him during the years of struggle leading to success. His is the ever recurring story of the successful man unable to step aside and to accept the painful verdict of time.

In a sudden crisis, although unwell for many months, Pinero was rushed to the Marylebone Nursing Home near his London residence. The emergency operation proved unsuccessful, and he died on November 23, 1934.

The Memorial Service was held in St. Marylebone Parish Church, York Gate, on the following Wednesday morning at eleven-thirty. Following the hymn, "O God, Our Help in Ages Past," the sentences were pronounced and the Twenty-third Psalm was read. The prayers were offered. After the singing of "Lead Kindly Light," Tennyson's "Crossing of the Bar" was read; then the benediction.

IX

PINERO'S CONTRIBUTION

THE modern critic, whether he holds a responsible position or merely enjoys the theater, should be wary of judging plays which he has not seen in the theater. For plays written for the theater should be tested in the theater. Words intended for oral delivery, their phrasing, and their suitability for quick transmission to the audience may seem obvious if not dull on the printed page. On the other hand, literary achievements may be better appreciated in the study.

The reader judges a play as literature, seldom if ever picturing in his mind's eye the scene on the stage, listening to voices in his imagination, or creating as he reads the movement and stage business. The reader too often assumes that the playwright finishes the creation, whereas anyone experienced in the theater knows well that the playscript leaves much for the production. But actors know the difference between the dialogue of a literary man and that of a playwright. The playwright's lines can be spoken with emphasis; the literary man's lines require no additional interpretation.

Much of the nonsense which passes, temporarily to be sure, as brilliant, eclectic criticism would not be written if these simple facts were considered.

The reading of the first-night reviews of all Pinero's plays and those written by his contemporaries leaves no doubt in mind whatsoever about the importance of his contribution between 1880 and 1910. Nor can I believe that any fair-minded critic who has read those reviews would disagree. The difficulty is that those reviews form a considerable body of material, not to be read by the critics who need that point of view.

The debonaire may smile and cast a devastating phrase about

99

rococo standards of the gas-lighted theaters. In so doing, however, they restrict the validity of their judgment to the contemporary stage. And I trust it is not critical heresy for one who has closely observed the theater for twenty years to suggest that the period from 1890 to 1910 was more exciting than from 1920 to 1940. But Henry Arthur Jones recognized the importance of his era, pointing out definitely in his now almost forgotten book, *The Renascence of the English Drama*, what features merited recognition.

But the substitution of social, economic, and political protests for the old-fashioned and abstract moral protests and the overuse of the protest against the double standard have contributed new points of view for dramatic criticism, from which the playwrights of the 1890's appear particularly out of date.

A century from now, when the facts upon which this estimate is based become obscured, Pinero will probably seem no more old fashioned than Clifford Odets or William Saroyan. Then, perhaps, the summing-up can be made with authority. But at the moment the present writer can only adduce the evidence as he sees it and be described as a reactionary. Be that as it may, the record is important.

From the historical consideration the case for Pinero can scarcely be overstated. He was the pioneer among his contemporaries, though he usually gave the credit to T. W. Robertson. Granville-Barker, in the Preface to *The Eighteen-seventies* ([Cambridge, 1929], p. xi), wrote understandingly of Pinero's contribution. In these essays by the Fellows of the Royal Society of Literatures is to be found Pinero's description of the drama as he found it and his acknowledgment of Robertson's leadership. But Pinero studied dramaturgy by writing plays and studying them in production. He took the formula of the *pièce bien faite* but emphasized characterization rather than plotting. He was fundamentally concerned with people, in particular with their mistakes. And he early developed a rather harsh philosophy for that age of sentiment by insisting upon the cause for every effect. This deterministic philosophy opposed the popularly advocated freedom of the will.

In his essay, "Robert Louis Stevenson: The Dramatist" (*Critic*, XLII [1909], 341 ff.), Pinero sharply differentiated between dramatic and theatric talent. His statement has become the classic differentiation between these two misunderstood expressions. The dramatic talent expresses itself in telling a story in dialogue, but the theatrical talent shapes that dialogue for effective stimulation of the audience's emotions in the theater.

In his essay, "Browning as a Dramatist" (*Transactions of the Royal Society of Literature*, Vol. XXXI, Part IV), presented on Browning's centenary, May 7, 1912, Pinero continued his discussion of theatrical talent, pointing out Browning's unwillingness to consider the requirements of the stage. As a result Browning's plays required more analysis and reflection than was permitted to the audience in the theater.

In the Foreword to *Two Plays* (London, 1930) Pinero lamented the intrusion of the producer between the playwright and his script. For Pinero believed that the playwright should stage-manage his own play, even as he had the majority of his plays.

But Pinero's painstaking attention to the details of production was not common in his heyday. In the *Era* for June 3, 1893, occurred an interview with Sir George Alexander, shortly after the première of *The Second Mrs. Tanqueray*. The interviewer sought information concerning Pinero's methods. Alexander replied that the play was produced precisely in every detail as indicated on the manuscript, except for eight words of dialogue.

When the interviewer asked Sir George to compare Pinero's script with that of Oscar Wilde's *Lady Windermere's Fan*, which had been very popular, Sir George explained that he had worked and argued to no end with Wilde about various points of production, in particular about Wilde's unwillingness to disclose the identity of Mrs. Erlynne; that on the opening night the play had almost failed; and that only then could he persuade Wilde to consider the spectator's problem.

Some playgoers of Pinero's heyday hold that he will be remembered for his farces at the Court Theatre. They saw those plays, as I have not. The magic of his stagecraft was certainly displayed in those early comedies of sentiment with their individual tang of cynicism, but only revivals of them can test that opinion; nevertheless, only the ignorant can deny the popularity of those comedies with the survivors of the audiences for whom the Court Farces were written and produced. And Pinero himself often reiterated his belief that a dramatist's work should be judged in accordance with the standards of the age for which he wrote.

Among the plays of moral protest *The Second Mrs. Tanqueray*, *The Notorious Mrs. Ebbsmith*, *Iris*, *His House in Order*, *The Thunderbolt*, and *Mid-Channel*, arbitrarily selected from those written between 1892 and 1909, represented for the present writer the height of Pinero's attainment. Their appeal is not limited to the era in which they were written. These characters and their problems, the philosophy, and the stagecraft are not limited by time and place. Three of these plays, *The Second Mrs. Tanqueray*, *The Thunderbolt*, and *Mid-Channel*, have already won their places in collections of modern drama. The other three merit as serious consideration, though obviously they are not as suitable for college classes.

In conclusion, Pinero's interests were not large. He disregarded the new social movements. He saw people as individuals, not as groups. But as master of dramaturgy and stagecraft he repays serious study and appreciation.

X

PINERO'S PHILOSOPHY

THE prevalent notion that Pinero was Victorian in his philosophy is utterly false. He had nothing whatsoever to do with Browning's declaration of the Christian faith; nor was he racked with doubt, as were Tennyson and Matthew Arnold. Though he posed not at all as a philosopher, he had a fixed point of view on life, scientific in its emphasis upon cause and effect, strikingly advanced for his time. But Shaw represented himself as a thinker, a creative evolutionist, a prophet in the wilderness, and wrote long prefaces and essays expounding his views. And Jones, too, wrote essays but floundered in his thinking between the dictates of his Puritan conscience and his disillusionment over hypocrisy within the church.

In what kind of world do Pinero's characters live? This question is fundamental to the understanding of the plays, indicating after production in the theater is past what the reader may hope to gain from them. For the reader is not carried away by the illusion created on the stage; he must build in his mind that illusion. And the playwright's philosophy thus becomes of primary concern. What forces shape the characters? How do the characters face the struggle of life? For if the drama depends upon conflict between characters or between the leading character and his environment, then the points of view on these conflicts hold significance.

Pinero took himself seriously. He did not depend upon the fortuitous development of circumstances; he struggled to prepare himself and make his own future. Everything that he did seemed to him to lead to something else, to be indicative of the future. For his time he was downright materialistic; the spiritual goal was secondary, if not neglected. The Cinderella theme could not appeal to him. Luck, good fortune, benevolent influences, were all beyond his reckoning.

Even in his early farce comedies his characters fail to attain their objectives because of some mistake earlier in their lives. Though they have hopes and sentiments, their judgment, physical condition, and limitations of environment eventually bring about frustration, since they are the kind of people they are. Stated in philosophical terms this is determinism. The psychological and physiological factors in their personalities make them thus and so; not fate, not the conjunction of their stars, not the wrath of God.

Pinero's simplest comedies are strikingly based on the sentiments of his characters rather than plot, however weak at times appear the characters. They make their own mistakes leading to frustration, exposure, and the peculiar embarrassment fundamental to Pinero's theory of comedy. Though in his ironic comedies and tragedies he permits the audience to sympathize with the plights of his characters so that the audience will not laugh at them but feel with them the absolute futility of striving for happiness, his characters recognize that happiness cannot be based upon a miserable foundation; that the future is only the past, no matter how an individual may strive to atone for past errors and struggle to redeem himself.

For Pinero's early contemporaries this cold, dispassionate, irreligious point of view was distinctly unpleasant, but he maintained it, and finally it became fashionable. But by that time Pinero's plays had lost favor, and many critics wrote of Pinero's lack of a settled philosophy.

Pinero was neither a fatalist nor a predestinarian; no exterior force molds the destiny of his characters. They all find, as later did Barrie's characters in *Dear Brutus*, that a second choice would not be different from the original, being the kind of persons they are. But Barrie invariably postulated the belief that the spirit could dominate the physical; that, in the words of Milton, the mind could make a heaven of hell, a hell of heaven. Barrie's greatest comedies are based on the premise that the world is as the characters would like to have it. For example, *Quality Street* represents the dream-come-true type of world; *Alice-Sit-by-the-Fire* reveals adults willing to accept the point of view of adolescence; *The Admirable Crichton*, for half its action, takes place amid a social cataclysm; and *Mary Rose* and *Peter Pan* exist in the illusions of childhood. But Pinero's comedies have no philosophy of escape.

The philosophy at the turn of the century most popular to Englishmen involved religious controversy. But only in *The Notorious Mrs. Ebbsmith* did Pinero discuss religion. And there he did so because the chief character was formerly a street preacher in London and represented an unorthodox attitude. When she meets the Reverend Amos Winterfield of the Church of England, she is disillusioned. The clergyman explains that his sister was saved by the mercy of heaven from leaving her husband. But Agnes, whose lover is about to desert her, cries out in anguish that if that miracle should happen to her, she would lose the last sustaining comfort to be got from life. Here is the universal cry of humanity for what it wants but cannot have.

In the end, however, Agnes sends her lover back to his wife, promising to pray for him when she has again learned how. Does Pinero suggest in this poignant scene that Agnes' contrition, necessary for prayer, will enable her to forgive Lucas for leaving her? I think not. Here is the basic principle of Pinero's philosophy: the utter hopelessness of the individual to change. Agnes' love for Lucas was predicated on her being a particular person. Through separation and suffering she may hope to, but never will, find solace in prayer. Someone else might, but not Agnes.

The Notorious Mrs. Ebbsmith created a furor among churchmen because, in the midst of Agnes' conversation with the clergyman, she hurls the Bible he has given her into the fire. This action was strictly in character, revealing the impulsiveness of her character. But Bibles are not burned on the stage. Even though she did thrust her hand into the stove to retrieve the Bible, its charred pages were symbolic of her sacrifice of every convention for personal happiness.

Clergymen appear in *The Hobby-Horse* and *Dandy Dick*, but they do not engage in religious debates. On the other hand, Jones wrote two of his most successful plays, *Saints and Sinners* and *Michael and His Lost Angel*, around religious controversies. And Shaw presented satirical sketches of orthodox religion in *Androcles and the Lion* and in *Back to Methuselah*. In particular, however, in *Candida* the clergyman with social welfare at heart is presented as weaker than a maladjusted poet. But Shaw himself informed me that *Saint Joan* was merely the biography of a real girl, thus dismissing the religious implications.

In pursuing this relentless philosophy of cause and effect, Pinero created characters who do not moan to high heaven or curse their fate. They seem to think for themselves, to realize and to perceive why things happen to them. Thus they become self-reliant though disillusioned. Confronted with choice, they invariably take the cash and let the credit go. They are not and cannot be idealists in the sense that they choose the hard way, sacrificing present pleasure for future happiness. For this reason the Victorian critics found Pinero without a philosophy. The truth is, these critics simply disliked what they found.

In the present scientific era, however, the simplest of men plant hybrid seeds and ignore the almanac of their fathers. If the seed is right and the conditions controlled, the plant will be determined, quite independent of fate or choice. Chemical and physical reactions which were miracles or the results of chance can now be predicted. And so to human beings comes the realization that experience cultivates the individual within the limits of his capacity. But the human factor of will-power, which Pinero strangely ignored, remains the great undeterminate.

Pinero's philosophy consequently seems more negative than it is because he selected people for his plays who lacked strength of will. His characters invariably fail to meet their responsibilities. That is his chief weakness as a philosopher. For in actual life he himself illustrated the principle that a man willing to sacrifice everything for a single objective can achieve success far beyond any prediction based upon his talent and education could hold for him.

Had Pinero created strong characters, his plays would have been inspirational rather than depressing. But he did not seek out the exceptional men and women; his characters are not heroic, except in their ability to suffer defeat unmitigated with hope. His view of man was cynical and bitter, based on the assumption of the prevailing weakness of man. And for this reason, more than any other, audiences and readers alike turned from the ideas in his plays to the stagecraft; from the unpleasant to the amusing.

If and as Pinero's plays come to be more widely read, his philosophy of cause and effect, determinism, and cynical rationalism will receive recognition for its clarity, firmness, and forthrightness, despite the limitations he imposed upon it through the selection of characters without will-power.

The *raisonneurs*, those understanding gentlemen who present to the perplexed characters the author's point of view, represent Pinero's philosophy. These omniscient fellows, like Cayley Drummle, Hilary Jesson, and Peter Mottram, look beyond the present to the future and in their expression of the long view emphasize Pinero's philosophy of conduct with an eye to the future. It is a practical matter, like honesty is the best policy. This materialistic attitude hardly spins itself into a theory, but it is a fixed view of life, a philosophy, whether admirable or not.

In *The Second Mrs. Tanqueray*, for example, Tanqueray objects to Cayley's suggesting the similarity between the reputations, the past lives of the new Lady Orreyed and Paula Ray; then Cayley says that he himself is only a spectator, like a man in the theater, but he wants to see certain persons happy in the end. It is Cayley, furthermore, who advises Tanqueray to permit Ellean to travel and to hope that in so doing she will find someone who will complete her life with happiness.

In *His House in Order*, Hilary Jesson reminds his brother that it is wrong to expect the special qualities of one woman in another—those of Annabel in Nina. And he suggests that the difficulty with marriage is that the husband wants his wife to accommodate herself to his interests, whereas he fails to adapt himself to hers. And, finally, it is Hilary who urges Nina to give up using her discovery about Annabel as a means of avenging herself on her husband and on Annabel's family. People who use power uncharitably, says Hilary, are never happy. But the people who conquer that temptation and sacrifice themselves find happiness in the end.

In *Mid-Channel* Peter argues with Zoe and Theodore to be patient with each other. He describes the middle years of marriage as similar to a rough crossing of the English Channel. Halfway across, the shoal causes the swift current to become excessively rough and unpleasant, but once the other side is reached the water is serene.

All three of these bachelors offer to their married friends sound, practical advice. Their advice, however, may be so obvious that it is not appreciated. Indeed, Pinero's philosophy lacks pretentiousness and deals with realities rather than ideals; certainly it is as usable today as when he set it down on the manuscript of his play.

XI

PINERO'S PORTRAYAL OF WOMEN

THE brilliance of Ibsen's galaxy of heroines has quite eclipsed in critical consideration the portraits of any other author at the close of the nineteenth century. Even the women of Hardy's novels, and Meredith's consummate delineation of Diana, create less enthusiasm, critical and popular. But Pinero's portrayal of women merits much more consideration than it has received, particularly as a realistic representation of the developing new woman in England.

In *The Madras House*, Granville-Barker has given the basis for comparing the Victorian girl surrounded by all the taboos and conventions of Victorian morality. But the plight of the Misses Huxtables was not particular; rather it was the experience of any well-born young women. Poor, gentle creatures, they languished in stuffy drawing-rooms until some proper young man offered them the bliss of marriage. But young men who brought only love were distinctly ineligible, however exciting the life they offered.

The rise of the middle class through manufacturing and merchandising to power and wealth extended to the daughters. Some sought education and careers in professions heretofore held sacrosanct to men; the majority merely sought freedom from the old, stifling conventions. Unprepared as the majority were by training and experience to realize that the new freedom brought responsibilities, they merely became notorious.

Pinero's experience in the theater as an actor gave him a point of view on the rise of the new woman, for the middle-class girls were now merely adopting the freedom long enjoyed by actresses. He consequently was not horrified by these excesses in deportment but rationalized whether the end attained justified the means. He was primarily concerned with the individual's defiance of society, for he well knew the consequences of such defiance in the lives of theater people, and society had not kept pace with the rapid development of its leaders in this new direction.

The mystery of the eternal feminine had become plain as a pikestaff—an exciting reality opening up new situations for plots and new characters for portrayal. To call Pinero's plays dated in this respect is merely to acknowledge the general abandonment of the Victorian standards of morality. For Pinero seemed to many of the first reviewers rather advanced in his attitude. In fact he was obviously regarded as shocking to the finer sensibilities of his time. But fifty years have brought unbelievable changes in freedom, if one takes the present Broadway season of 1940–41 as a basis for comparison.

Pinero's first heroine of any consequence is Leslie Brudenell in *The Profligate*. In type she is the old-fashioned, sheltered product of the Victorian code of morality. When she faces life she is horrified to discover that her husband has had an affair with a girl whom she has befriended. Her importance is her femininity; she actually possesses the point of view of a Victorian innocent in all she says and does. However much of a prig she may appear to the modern girl, the fact is that Pinero understood her and sympathized with her. He might have satirized her and ridiculed her ideals, but he depicts her quite realistically. And writing convincing dialogue for women to speak is an accomplishment not often to be observed in the work of many authors distinguished in other respects.

Though Leslie may seem selfish, too ready to misunderstand her profligate husband, Camilla Brent, Pinero's next portrait, exhibits generosity to the extreme. She is called "Lady Bountiful." As a matter of fact she merits the description, for she too is a paragon of virtue but in addition is willing to forgive.

When Dennis Heron marries beneath him, the daughter of a riding master, Camilla is grievously disappointed, for Margaret seems unworthy of Dennis' love. Camilla appears aloof and superior; not as liberal in her attitude as she is with her money. In characterization, however, this weakness of Camilla marks an important advance in Pinero's capacity for delineating women. Leslie Brudenell was too perfect, despite her self-righteousness. Camilla appears more human and more attractive, though she transgresses no social standard. On the other hand, Margaret, Dennis' wife, ill bred, crude, and limited though she is, wins respect because of her sincere love for Dennis. She sacrifices everything for Dennis' happiness and before she dies assures herself that Camilla will accept Dennis.

Pinero had before him the simple formula of a well-born but penniless young man in love with an heiress but married to a common girl of the streets. But the old triangle is cast aside through the realistic portrayal of character so that Dennis chooses not at all between a good and a bad woman but finds admirable characteristics and weaknesses in both. The barrier of class distinction and the need to make a living frustrate the happiness that Dennis and Margaret snatch from life.

The significant feature of these characterizations lies in Pinero's representation of two opposing viewpoints. Margaret realizes that though she has married Dennis she can possess only a part of him; the rest belongs to Dennis' first though unexpressed love for Camilla. On the other hand, Camilla knows throughout Dennis' brief marriage to Margaret that within her own heart she holds a part of Dennis quite unpossessed by Margaret. But Pinero does not make this distinction on the basis of sex. It is because each girl through her individual experience can offer something the other does not have that produces the conflict in the play. Basically it is the conflict between wealth and poverty and what these conditions of life have done to these two girls. Both are finer and nobler in these circumstances than either could be if the conditions were reversed. In other words, Camilla in Margaret's situation and Margaret in Camilla's situation would lack attractiveness. Their respective environments have developed them.

Paula Tanqueray ranks as Pinero's greatest achievement, if the long line of distinguished actresses who have sought to play her role means anything at all. And Paula is one of the few among

Pinero's heroines who change and become transformed within the limits of the play. As a matter of fact few heroines in all the drama change. The dramatist has insufficient time for such delineation as the novelist can give. So when a character in a play becomes transformed, the occasion is noteworthy.

Opposite Paula is her stepdaughter, Ellean, convent reared, intolerant, and suspicious. But Paula wants Ellean's love more than even the life of respectability which she has sought in marrying Tanqueray. In fact her desire for Ellean's respect aids Paula to strive on when the neighbors and friends of the first Mrs. Tanqueray snub her. Then it is that the audience realizes how much Paula has changed from the lighthearted, luxury-loving, irresponsible toast of the Riviera into the cautious and defensive stepmother.

In the pitiable defense of herself against Ellean's upbraiding over the matter of intercepting Ellean's letters to her father, Paula struggles forlornly to hold Ellean's love, but Paula's past life with Captain Hugh Ardale, who now wishes to marry Ellean, establishes the problem. Paula has to choose between concealing her past indiscretion and telling Ellean and Aubrey the truth; to keep silent and hold Ellean's love is the temptation which Paula is able to overcome; in so doing, however, she sacrifices the love not only of Ellean but of her husband, the only man who has ever been kind to her. Hence, with loss of love Paula now cannot face life and so destroys herself. But a few months before her marriage she would have lightly sought another lover to support her. That is the evidence of her transformation.

Iris could understand Paula's attitude, but Iris lacked Paula's strength and did not change. Iris wants young Trenwith's love, despite giving herself to Maldonado. She lacks the essential honesty of Paula. This is the primary difference between these two luxury-loving young women. But Iris is honest with herself in the last scene with Trenwith, when she admits her weakness, her willingness to sacrifice everything for security during Trenwith's absence.

Zoe Blundell belongs with Iris and Paula as transgressors of the moral code. Zoe, however, is more responsible for her problem than the others. For Paula's indiscretions take place before the play begins, when she was young and without guidance, and her sincere desire to adopt the conventional way of life makes her wrongdoing appear less reprehensible. In fact, during the play Paula does nothing immoral except to intercept Ellean's letters. Iris yields to Maldonado's demands because she has lost her fortune, and Trenwith, far away in Australia, offers little hope for her future. She is merely weak. But Zoe deliberately leaves her husband and invites Leonard Ferris to come to her in Italy. Whatever excuses may be made for Paula and Iris, nothing mitigates Zoe's mistake. She wilfully involves herself in an affair which she knows will eventually reach her husband's attention. In fact she wants to hurt Theodore, to arouse his jealousy. Each one of these three pleasure-loving women has a different personality, an individual motive, and a particular problem arising from lewdness.

The nearest to them in type is Theo in *The Benefit of the Doubt*, but she is merely careless of her reputation. The correspondent named by her husband in the divorce action appears comparatively innocent, not a little bored by her attentions.

Agnes, the notorious Mrs. Ebbsmith, wants to hold her lover, the husband of another woman, but her reputation is not at stake for the simple reason that she cares only for her lover. Here again Pinero supplies just as convincing motives for her attitude as for those of his other heroines. Agnes had not found happiness in conventional marriage, though she was idealistic about it. Now she struggles to wrest from an unconventional union not physical pleasure but intellectual companionship. In the end she yields herself in order to hold Lucas Cleeve from returning to his wife. The fact that both Lucas and his wife have no affection for each other and that their reunion is merely for appearances directs the sympathy of the audience to Agnes. Her affair seems less sordid than the hypocritical marriage.

The most sinned against of all Pinero's leading women is Nina in *His House in Order*. She is the second wife of Filmer Jesson, who worships the memory of his first wife, the sainted Annabel. Nina suffers not only from Filmer's constantly reminding her of her shortcomings but from Derek, Annabel's son, and all of Annabel's relatives. When by chance Nina has the opportunity to expose Annabel's adultery, to reveal that Derek is not Jesson's son, Nina is strong enough to be persuaded by Jesson's brother not to revenge herself. Nina thus becomes the only one of Pinero's heroines not to be the victim of her own mistakes; she alone suffers from the faults of others.

Rose Trelawny, in *Trelawny of the "Wells,"* and Sophy Fullgarney, the loyal manicurist in *The Gay Lord Quex*, are both from the lower middle class. But the problems they encounter are solved so that they remain young idealists. On the other hand, Letty, a shopgirl, decides against marriage with her employer and an affair with the wealthy Letchmere, who has a wife, and finally marries a young photographer of her own class. Despite her protestations to Letchmere that she is happy, Pinero does not make her situation very attractive. Her conventional marriage seems dull, indeed, when contrasted with the exciting life she might have had with Letchmere.

Phyllis Mortimore and Helen Thornhill in *The Thunderbolt* represent the ultimate achievement of Pinero in depicting normal, middle-class women uninvolved in sexual problems. Phyllis is a housewife and mother who destroys a will in order that her children may benefit from their uncle's estate. Ironically enough, the property was left to Helen Thornhill, the illegitimate daughter of the deceased Edward Mortimore. This recognition meant much to Helen, for Phyllis is the only one among the Mortimores who treats Helen with friendliness. Helen tries to forgive Phyllis, who confesses her crime. Thus Helen shares somewhat the nobility which sets Nina apart from other Pinero heroines. Phyllis' act is motivated by the Mortimores' mistreatment of her and of her husband as well as by her desire to have her children profit. Her mistake is a matter of misjudgment, of failure to realize that she was breaking the law, and of her assumption that the estate belonged to the Mortimores, not to the unknown girl designated in the will. But her mistake is wilfully made. The ironical aspect is not in her so doing, but in her liking the girl she cheated, when Helen Thornhill arrives.

These illustrations of the scope of Pinero's portrayal of women indicate certainly that he was not content to deal with women merely as types. Luxury-loving transgressors of the moral code, perplexed but inherently honest shopgirls, and misunderstood wives are terms insufficient to describe them. The careful motivation of each decision and act develops their characters to the point that they seem actually to have lived in one's experience.

By contrast consider Pinero's delineation of men. Though highly individualized, his men may be readily typed. The baffled husband, for example, includes Aubrey Tanqueray, Filmer Jesson, Thaddeus Mortimore, and Theodore Blundell. Or take the young lovers who cannot earn a living, such as Dennis Heron, Laurence Trenwith, and Leonard Ferris. The roué, or man-about-town, like Lord Quex, the Duke of St. Olpherts, and Lord Dangars. And, finally, there are the understanding bachelors— Cayley Drummle, Hilary Jesson, and Peter Mottram. Within their types any of these characters could be substituted for another without serious change in the precise delineation of characteristics.

None of Pinero's women discussed in this account could possibly be substituted for another. Paula would not make Zoe's mistake. Paula's problem would not disturb Iris at all. Agnes Ebb-smith could not sympathize with any of these women. Nina would have scorned them as hypocrites. Letty was too virtuous to become so involved. Each of these women is a personality confronted eventually with a problem of her own making, either directly or indirectly the result of her earlier decisions and actions.

It is fair to say that none of Pinero's heroines is wholly admirable. Each has her peculiar faults, fails to find happiness, and in the end compromises her hopes and ideals. As a result one leaves the theaters or lays down the book with the feeling that Pinero's women are not fiction but closely observed from life. They are heir to all the foibles harassing human beings. They speak and act like ordinary people.

If these women lack commanding respect and noble emotions, they at least represent faithfully the life which they led. Pinero saw good in women of ill-repute as well as evil in those of virtuous reputation. His frankness in describing human beings as he saw them must be his weakness, but it is not an artistic fault.

APPENDIX I

MERELY PERSONAL

The fact that Pinero had always refused to grant interviews justifies my describing my experiences and my meetings with him. Although I did not talk with him until February, 1934, and he died the following November, those talks gave me a point of view on his lifetime devoted to the theater.

I first read *The Second Mrs. Tanqueray* while I was in college and then read rapidly as many more of his plays as were available, finding his bitter cynicism much to my personal liking. But a decade was to pass before I had the time to begin a serious study of his plays and the theater of his time.

In the autumn of 1933, however, my studies had progressed to the point that I needed more information than had been published about him, and I wrote him, telling of my interest in his work. He replied as follows:

> 115 A HARLEY STREET, W. 1.
> 21st. November, 1933

MY DEAR SIR,

Thank you for your kind letter. I cannot tell you anything about myself beyond what appears in the books of reference. Self-advertising in any form is not to my taste.

I am sending you a book published in 1930, of which I beg your acceptance. The Foreword may be of some little use to you.

Believe me

> Yours most truly
> ARTHUR PINERO

The Foreword proved of little assistance, except to reveal a rather crotchety temper, a little ill at ease in neglect, amid the changed conditions in the London theaters. As for books of reference, as too frequently is the case, they merely repeated the

clichés and misreported facts of early writers handicapped by
Pinero's lack of co-operation.

I wrote Sir Arthur that I would be in London on sabbatic leave
early in February and would appreciate an opportunity to pay
him my respects. To that optimistic observation I received no
reply whatsoever. On arriving in London, however, I immediately wrote him my address. By return mail came a courteous invitation to call two mornings hence and an apology for the delay
owing to his illness. This was more satisfactory than the note I
had received the previous autumn in America.

The prospect of meeting Sir Arthur brought doubts, for I had
a stack of manuscript notes which lacked significance unless he
proved to be more communicative and co-operative than seemed
possible. If no basis for mutual understanding could be established, my sabbatic leave would seem a failure.

He lived at 115 A Harley Street, London, but his house was
actually located in Devonshire Street, owing to the amazing system of house-numbering in London. This is a pleasant neighbor-
hood, just south of Regent's Park. Harley Street is of course well
known for its lodgings of medical specialists. Indeed, the cabby
asked me if I sought a doctor. To the west is Wimpole Street,
familiar to students of poetry. For at No. 50 lived Elizabeth Bar-
rett, when Browning wooed and subsequently eloped with her.
At No. 67 had lived Arthur Hallam, whom Tennyson visited in
boyhood and about whom Tennyson wrote *In Memoriam.*

Pinero's house was Georgian, built of rose-colored brick, set off
from the other houses. The walls of the other houses joined, individuality indicated only by the architectural treatment of the
entrances.

My knock at the door was answered. I was ushered through
the center hall and up the stairway to his study. He came to meet
me; his large eyes brightened with his smile. Heavy set, broad
shouldered, he appeared more like a man who had spent his days
out of doors rather than in the study or theater. But the most
noticeable feature was his eyebrows: long tufts, they jutted
straight out from his bald, egg-shaped head. His large eyes, large

nose, large mouth, gave the impression of strength. His skin was taut and firm. He was quick in his movements. Had I not known he was seventy-eight and in a few months would celebrate another birthday, I should have assumed he was twenty years younger.

The enormous vitality which had spurred him on to write over fifty full-length plays impressed itself upon me. He spoke rapidly and without the slightest diffidence. "I'm glad to see you. You know, I've been ill. I'm just a wreck of a man now. My secretary thought I shouldn't see anyone, but I wanted to see you. A young man who would bring a year-old baby across the Atlantic in mid-winter interests me. I'm glad you've come. What may I do to help you? Are you well located? Are Mrs. Dunkel and the children all right? They stood the trip? Now, just where is it you are living?"

These questions cascaded into my mind. But before I could reply, he was asking, "Why do you want to write a book about me, about my plays?" And I replied, "Because you wrote *The Second Mrs. Tanqueray*, and I can find out so little about you."

He smiled quickly and nodded as if in assent. Then, after a moment's hesitation he began asking me about the progress of my work. He seemed surprised that anyone wishing to write a book about a living author should take the trouble to read all that the author had written. And when I explained that I proposed to spend the next three months in reading through the dramatic criticism on file in Colindale Branch of the British Museum, he exclaimed, "Good! I will help you all I can."

Then he crossed to his desk and returned with the correspondence between himself and Hamilton Fyfe, the distinguished English critic who had written two books about Sir Arthur.

"Have you read Hamilton Fyfe's books?"

I told him that I had done so and disagreed with Mr. Fyfe's interpretations rather heartily.

"Good!" exclaimed Sir Arthur, again. "You have an opportunity to correct some misstatements of fact as well as of opinion. Mind you, I don't care what he says about the plays. They will have to stand for themselves. But the facts about myself must be corrected."

He handed me an envelope containing the correspondence. Herewith I reproduce them, not to disparage Mr. Fyfe's work, but to indicate the difficulty involved in previous attempts to establish facts about Sir Arthur and his work. For the sake of the record these corrections should be made. Fortunate, indeed, was I that Sir Arthur had mellowed and at last realized the need to co-operate.

115 A, HARLEY STREET, W. 1.
13th. May, 1930

DEAR HAMILTON FYFE,

Reading the opening chapter of your book last night, I almost had a fit. Who on earth has been imposing on you those stories of my Lyceum days? Utterly false, every one of them. I had too great a regard for Irving—to say nothing of the awe in which I held him—to treat him with pertness and familiarity. And as for the sticking of an impudent notice on the call-board by a member of the company, such an outrageous proceeding would have brought disgrace upon the offender, and perhaps summary dismissal. The theatre was strictly conducted and its rules reverently obeyed. In that respect I may have been influenced by my association with Irving; in no other way, I think.

I was not present at the first performance of "The Bells," nor have I ever acted Sir Peter Teazle at the Haymarket or elsewhere.

My father practised in South Square, Gray's Inn, in Prince's Street (since renamed), Bedford Row, and in Great James Street, never in Lincoln's Inn Fields.

I was born at No. 21 Dalby Terrace, Islington, then a pleasant enough locality—not in the Old Kent road or the Seven Dials.

I am wondering whether, for the sake of my peace of mind, I dare read any further.

Forgive this outbreak, and believe me,

Yours always,
ARTHUR PINERO

BESSEL'S GREEN, SEVENOAKS, KENT.
May 15 1930.

DEAR SIR ARTHUR

I am so sorry you have been annoyed by inaccuracies. You will remember that I once asked you if you could give me any information about your life and you preferred not to do so. I was therefore driven back on other sources, mostly books of reminiscences and newspaper articles. I supposed that if these had contained inaccuracies, you would have had them corrected at the time. Many of the stories about the Lyceum days came, I understand, from old Mr. Howe and other old stagers of Irving's company. Of course I will correct anything that you tell me is wrong if we have a second edition of the book. But it would be a pity to worry about them. I never read anything that is written about me. I know it will be for the most part wrong. But what does it matter? It seems very strange, by the way, that Percy Fitzgerald mentioned your playing Sir Peter in a book of his. What tricks memory can play us!

Sincerely,

HAMILTON FYFE

115 A, HARLEY STREET, W. 1.
17th May, 1930.

DEAR HAMILTON FYFE,

Thank you for your light-hearted letter. I have no recollection of your asking me to give you particulars of my life, I understand that your book was to be a critical survey of my work; that and nothing more. This is clearly suggested by your title—"Sir A. P.'s Plays and Players." If I had thought you had intended to go further I should either have begged you to abandon the idea or have put myself to the pains of supplying you with details. You must forgive me for saying that my refusal to furnish you with facts, if I ever did so, is no justification for raking together, and accepting without question, the stuff written by other people.

What does it matter? I have always acted on the principle that everything matters; but, then, I am much your senior, and was brought up in a stupid, old-fashioned school.

Please don't bother to acknowledge this.

Sincerely yours,

ARTHUR PINERO

Percy Fitzgerald! Good heavens! Fancy regarding that writer as an authority on any subject! He was notoriously inaccurate.

BESSEL'S GREEN, SEVENOAKS, KENT.
23 V 30

DEAR SIR ARTHUR

I have been trying to put my hand on the letter you wrote me when I wrote my first book about your work, in which you said you could not give me any particulars about yourself. I have not yet found it, but I shall do so, I expect. Anyway I recollect the terms of it quite well.

When I set to work on the second book, I knew it would be no use asking you to alter your decision, for I was aware that your horror of "publicity" had deepened in the interval.

No publisher would have looked at a study of the plays without some chapters of biography. There is no money in the book anyway. Benn may just clear expenses. I shall make nothing out of it, nor did I expect to. I had quite another motive in writing it.

To find the biographical details I went through all the volumes of stage memoirs published during the last thirty years or so. I included nothing that was not authenticated by someone's statement of what I believed to be fact. I am very sorry indeed that I have been deceived by some of these volumes. I had no means of knowing that Percy Fitzgerald was "notoriously inaccurate." He is generally accepted as an authority on theatrical history. It shows how one may be mistaken.

I am so sorry that my "light-heartedness" jarred on you. Believe me, this thing has worried me a lot. But after all the life of a book nowadays is little more than that of a newspaper article. Soon they are both forgotten and soon we all shall be. Which may be annoying or consoling, according to temperament.

I hope you won't mind me wishing you a Happy Birthday and many Happy Returns. Please do not trouble to answer this.

Sincerely,

HAMILTON FYFE

MOVABLE BIRTHPLACES

To the Editor of the " Times"

SIR,

With reference to the varying statements made by eminent people as to their place of birth, I may perhaps be pardoned for calling attention to another side of the picture—the departure from truth which is sometimes indulged in by self-appointed biographers in dealing, even in the lifetime of their subjects, not only with eminent persons, but, as in the instance I am now citing, with persons of no eminence whatever.

Not long ago a well-known author who thought it worth while to write a book about myself gave my birthplace as the Old Kent-road, and proceeded to enhance his statement by a description of the house in which that unimportant event took place. Upon my remonstrating with him on this inaccuracy and informing him that I was born in Islington, he cheerfully replied, "What does it matter?" I agree; in my case it matters little, except in so far as the Old Kent-road is concerned. The credit of the Old Kent-road should be maintained at all costs.

I am, Sir, yours faithfully,

ARTHUR PINERO

(The *Times*, Monday, July 27, 1931)

After reading these letters I realized for the first time the difficulties confronting me in the completion of my work. But I carried on my reading of the criticism in the newspapers and magazines. The early drafts of this book contained full quotations from these accounts in order to indicate the vogue of Pinero's plays and the wholehearted response of the critics to his work during the pre-war period. But editors of commercial publishing houses, casting about for some means to reject pleasantly my manuscript, to a man suggested that these elaborate quotations gave my manuscript the appearance of an old scrapbook. So four months of dismal copying have been discarded in this final draft.

This painstaking work, however, pleased Pinero, and he read my entire manuscript, writing in his own hand corrections, additions, and opinions along the margins. And to gain that close contact during the formative period of my writing this book may justify whatever seeming waste of time resulted later from discarding the first-night reviews.

Pinero's study was the largest room in the house. On either side of the fireplace were bookshelves; at either end of the room windows faced his garden and the street; there were windows opposite the fireplace. The walls, however, were hung with autographed portraits of the people who had made the theater of the eighteen-eighties and nineties.

His bookshelves contained the novels of Dickens, Thackeray, Scott, and Hardy. There were complete editions of Shakespeare, Molière, Congreve, and Robertson. But Pinero himself said that he was not an omnivorous reader.

His plays came from the streets, cafés, and well-to-do, middle-class homes. He was a photographer rather than a painter, always more concerned with details than with interpretation. Our talks concerned personalities and places rather than ideas.

Two summers after Pinero's death I returned to London and made the acquaintance of Mr. and Mrs. Claude Neville Hughes. Owing to their kindness and interest I am able to include additional facts and letters. In particular, however, I am indebted to Sir Arthur's secretary, Miss Eveleen Mills, not only for prompt attention to my requests but for kindly co-operation; to Dr. Robert F. Metzdorf, my former student and colleague; and to the University of Rochester for sabbatic leave. I wish also to acknowledge my appreciation of a grant-in-aid from the Council of Learned Societies.

APPENDIX II

EXTRACTS FROM THE FIRST-NIGHT REVIEWS

My original plan was to reproduce throughout this study of Sir Arthur Pinero all of the important newspaper and magazine reviews of the premières of his plays. To that end I copied them from these mediums on file in the Colindale Branch of the British Museum. The result was chaotic, giving to my manuscript the appearance of an old scrapbook of newspaper and magazine clippings. However impracticable my idea, the purpose was valid, for there I found the justification for my inferences about Pinero's plays. Those older critics held opinions diametrically opposed to the current judgment of present-day critics in many and high places.

The reprinting of a few reviews in this place is warranted by two considerations: namely, to give fuller expression than has seemed possible elsewhere to the taste and quality of those critics as indicated by their complete statements and to point out that Shaw's opinions of Pinero, widely copied by present-day critics, were not held by the other contemporaries of Pinero. Shaw's two volumes of *Dramatic Opinions and Essays* (New York, 1906) are so well known that I need not include them here. But, as William Archer observed in *The Drama Old and New*, Shaw did not become a critic until eighteen months after the première of *The Second Mrs. Tanqueray*. Shaw, however, lost no time in damning the play, and his opinion has held for those who have neither read nor seen it.

The following selected reviews reveal the critical standards according to which Pinero's plays developed.

William Archer in the *World* (May 1, 1889, pp. 8-9):

The next few weeks at the Garrick Theatre will be full of significance for the future of the English drama. If *The Profligate* succeeds—really and solidly succeeds—we shall know that there exists in England a public of men and women ready and even eager to accept the serious treatment of serious themes. . . . . I have long maintained that the supposed necessity for comic relief, happy endings, and so forth was a mere delusion. . . . . It is no secret that when Mr. Pinero wrote *The Profligate* he intended to print, not to produce it. The fear of the bogie was upon him; and had it not been for Mr. Hare's insight and courage, the triumph of Wednesday night might have been (at least) indefinitely postponed. . . . . Like all serious plays, it calls for examination from two points of view: the technical and the ethical. Technically, it shows a new development in Mr. Pinero's art, which has hitherto been distinguished rather by delicacy than by breadth of effect.

From the moment when we realize that Leslie, misinterpreting Janet's cry, takes Lord Dangars for the seducer, the scene becomes altogether tragic. I do not hesitate to call it the finest situation in the modern drama, the most thrilling, the most moving. We knew Mr. Pinero before as an inexhaustible humorist, an adroit theatrical craftsman, and a poet in his way; this scene reveals the accomplished, I had almost said the inspired, dramatist.

A. B. Walkley in the *London Times* (March 9, 1891):

The Haymarket has not long been allowed to remain in unique possession of a strong, original, unconventional English play significant of that latter-day renascence of English drama which we are all fain to acknowledge and to welcome. When, at the Garrick Theatre on Saturday night, the curtain fell on *Lady Bountiful*, the conviction was a general one in the house that Mr. Pinero had at length achieved in the serious vein a degree of success as has so often crowned his inventions in farce and comedy. For the author of *Lady Bountiful* has contrived to tell a tale, which is at once plausibly new and true, and which, if tinged with the gloom of real life, has also the elevating effect of a work of art. It is a play illustrative of cross-purpose, of thwarted aims, of unblushing selfishness, and noble endeavor, with an all-pervading suggestion of the divinity that shapes our ends, roughhew them as we will. Such a play is necessarily one of character chiefly, and character that does not run in the ordinary groove. The handful of literary puppets that dance to the piping of the commonplace playwright have no place here. Like his brilliant colleague at the Haymarket, Mr. Pinero has not thought it necessary to provide his story either with a hero or a villain; he has left it to poor human nature to work out its own evil and its own redemption. If the play has a moral at all, it is to teach the force of the principle which, in the language of the Hebrew prophet, "makes for righteousness" and which the modern German philosophy more abstrusely calls *das Unberwusste.* . . . .

The story thus told with the masterly touches of a dramatist of Mr. Pinero's caliber is one that sends the spectator home with conflicting and even painful

thoughts in his mind—thoughts of the vanity of human schemes in the presence
of the immensely larger and inscrutable forces that make or mar the lives of
men—Pessimism of the narrow Ibsen kind is depressing on the stage when it is
not merely irritating, but this of Mr. Pinero's has a wholesome influence; it is
not so much depressing as chasting. And very admirable is the acting. . . . .

A. B. Walkley in the *London Times* (May 29, 1893):

Measured, not by years, but by the march of events, the time is already far
distant when *La Dame aux camélias* stood in Lord Chamberlain's list of forbidden
plays; and there could be no better reminder of the change which has come over
the spirit of the English stage within the past ten or twelve years than the fact
that "the second Mrs. Tanqueray" can make her entrée on Mr. Pinero's arm
without preliminary announcement or apology. It was not so with the second
Mrs. Tanqueray's prototypes. As M. Dumas has always been rather prolific in
prefaces, he has naturally had much to say in defence of his glorification of the
demi-mondaine, but even M. Emile Augier thought it well to preface *Le Mariage
d'Olympe* with a few words in extenuation of his conduct in selecting his heroine
from a certain class. "Que peut la pudeur publique [he wrote] contre un fait
reconnu? Or, l'existence de ces demoiselles en est un. Elles ont passé des
régiones occultes de la société dans les régions avoriées. Elles ont pris droit de
cité dans les moeurs publiques." Had Mr. Pinero thought it necessary to apolo-
gize for introducing his latest heroine to our notice, he might have borrowed
textually Augier's preface to *Le Mariage d'Olympe*, set himself to controvert,
maintaining his counter thesis of *la nostalgie de la boue*. So far as he has cared to
join in the controversy Mr. Pinero ranges himself on the side of Augier. Most
probably, however, he has set out with no particular thesis; he has taken a type
of humanity which does undoubtedly exist; and without troubling himself to
tell the mother of "the young lady of fifteen" that the scope of her daughter's
education at the theatre in these days is apt, like Tom Weller's knowledge of
London, to be extensive and peculiar, he proceeds to develop that type in strict
accordance with the conditions of its environment. He has little concern indeed
with *la nostalgie de la boue*, which is not a special trait of the second Mrs. Tanqueray's character. He takes the fashionable adventuress who changes her name
almost as frequently as her gowns, gratifies her aspirations towards marriage,
places her in a good social position, and allows her to be choked and crushed to
death under her load of respectability. While pointing the same moral as *Le
Mariage d'Olympe*, *The Second Mrs. Tanqueray* is English and modern, and, in
justice to Mr. Pinero's talent be it said, a terribly lurid exposure of the theories
of M. Dumas. The new St. James's play may be unpleasant in its theme—this,
indeed, it is—and the rank taste which it leaves in the mouth may, and probably
will, militate against its general popularity; but it is written with undeniable
power, and is worked out to its tragic issue with a stern and inflexible logic

which fully atones for what may at first appear the somewhat gratuitous offer of the author to take his audience for a stroll in Regent-street by night. . . . .

Clement Scott in the *Daily Telegraph* (May 29, 1893):

Destiny, in point of fact, is not some external, cruel, and arbitrary power; destiny is nothing but our own characters. A man disappointed in one marriage and in one species of womanhood forms a second contract with a wife of diametrically opposite tendencies. . . . .

From another standpoint the new play presents the converse and complementary view of the one indicated by Alexandre Dumas in "La Dame aux Camélias." If the French dramatist tried to represent the real purity, *la virginité de l'âme*, which can be found in so world-stained a character as that of Marguerite Gautier, Mr. Pinero, with a truer insight into life and with less care for attractive stage pictures, tears off the fascinations of romance from his heroine, Paula, and shows her as she is—a woman who has made it impossible, both for herself and for those with whom she lives, to win peace. . . . .

At the same time, we have in these and similar passages a clear indication of the limitations under which Mr. Pinero has forced himself to work. The play is so strong and powerful that it would be difficult to find any English piece with which it ought properly to be compared, with the exception of the author's own companion story, "The Profligate." But the result of his resolute desire to be unflinchingly truthful is that there is no figure in his picture gallery that is sympathetic. . . . .

A. B. Walkley in the *London Times* (March 14, 1895):

It is not often given to an author to repeat himself with the degree of success which attended Mr. Pinero's new play, *The Notorious Mrs. Ebbsmith.* For there is in this latest heir of Mr. Pinero's invention something of repetition. Had not *The Second Mrs. Tanqueray* led the way, *The Notorious Mrs. Ebbsmith* would probably never have been written. The subject of the second play is less obvious, less daring, less dramatic than that of the first. Yet it travels along the same plane of morality, harasses the spectator with the same painful emotions, and finally enforces the same moral, which is that the conventions of society with regard to the marriage tie are not lightly to be set at defiance. Mrs. Tanqueray attempted marriage under unconventional conditions and failed at it. Mrs. Ebbsmith having found marriage a failure, tries a free and untrammelled union with the man whom she accepts as her affinity and fails in that equally. In both cases, the outraged conventions are avenged, but less signally, less plausibly, perhaps, in the second play than in the first. The experiment upon which Mrs. Ebbsmith embarks is one foredoomed to disaster. So much is evident almost from the opening scene, so that by the advocates of the "new morality" which Mr. Pinero condemns it may not unfairly be retorted that he does not give their system a chance. Mrs. Ebbsmith, who makes her appearance in the guise of a dowdy "new woman," in a plain brown dress with carelessly tied up hair, and destitute of all feminine attractions, tells her story in a few words.

The working of "rational marriage," or of the irregular bond, then, is the problem with which Mr. Pinero sets out, and the solution of which is the motive of the play. Mrs. Patrick Campbell, as Mrs. Tanqueray, proved herself an ideal representation of the social outcast, and it is she who is cast for the part of Mrs. Ebbsmith—a creation not less successful in its way. With her is Mr. Forbes-Robertson, who, as Lucas, is charged with the embodiment of a young man of aesthetic tastes and somewhat nebulous ideals, in which, perhaps, the regeneration of society occupies a smaller place than he suspects. Lucas still chafes at the thought of his matrimonial trammels, and is grateful to his new companion for having pulled him through his illness, but otherwise he betrays but small capacity for his task as a fellow-worker in "the cause." . . . . In an evil moment the clergyman's sister offers the disconsolate woman the consolation of the Bible. This is the last straw. Mrs. Ebbsmith, in a bitterly cynical speech which thrills the audience to their marrow, flouts the book in which she had already sought comfort without finding it, and throws it into the fire. Instantly, however, she repents of her action, and plunging her bare arm into the depths of the Italian stove, recovers the sacred volume and clasps it to her bosom as the act drop descends. The effect upon the house can only be described as electrical. This is perhaps the finest scene that Mr. Pinero has yet given us, and it is none the less so for being symbolical of the *dénouement* which he had in view. For the last act is, of course, concerned with the dissolution of the unfortunate union, the *scène d'faire* being the bringing of the wife and the mistress face to face, with the result that they mutually learn something of charity from each other. At the last moment Lucas would throw over society and its conventions and resume his irregular life. But Mrs. Ebbsmith is now resolved upon her own regeneration, in which she is promised the aid and support of the good clergyman and his sister.

William Archer in the *World* (March 14, 1895):

The *St. James's Gazette*, in an article headed "The Notorious Mr. Redford," argues that because Mr. Pinero's new play at the Garrick has been licensed, the Censorship is not practically repressive to dramatic literature. Ingenious St. James's! Does it really imagine that if *The Notorious Mrs. Ebbsmith* had been the work of an unknown writer, or, indeed, of any one but Mr. Pinero, it would have been licensed? Not a bit of it. This admirable work, which even Mr. Clement Scott hails as "a tragedy which brings out in its authorship and acting the very best that we have got in English art," would have been consigned to the limbo of still born improprieties.

The new play is in all essentials a great advance on *The Second Mrs. Tanqueray*. Those critics who take the opposite view are in reality hankering after the more

commonplace and melodramatic elements in the earlier play. In it we had
character precipitated by external coincidence; here we have character working
itself out entirely from within. Moreover, Mr. Pinero has here chosen a much
more vital theme. Most of us can afford to take a very abstract interest in the
theory of marriage with a demirep. We know in advance that it is a hazardous
experiment. . . . . In *The Notorious Mrs. Ebbsmith*, on the other hand, Mr.
Pinero goes straight for the universally relevant theme of marriage in general,
and draws three characters in place of one. . . . .

But love, in the largest sense of the word, is as uncomprehensible to them as
passion. They do not want either friendship or close companionship of a man.
Their interest is to make their own sex as nearly as possible self-sufficing. Why,
then, should they incur all sorts of social disadvantages for the sake of a companionship which they do not require or desire? And, in any case, Agnes is
clearly not a creature of this brood. She is not naturally a passionless woman.
She loves Lucas, in the fullest sense of the word, with a love that survives
even her fuller insight into his character. Her aspiration towards a "colder,
more temperate, more impassive companionship," is a merely intellectual
vagary; and I venture to think that it springs from a misconception on Mr.
Pinero's part. Newspaper moralists have so persistently prefixed the stereotyped
"sexless" and "unsexed" to the "new woman" that he has been betrayed into
grafting an inconsistent attribute upon his heroine's character. The real, or at
any rate the characteristic, "new woman" accepts with something more than
equanimity the destinies of her sex, and would certainly not ignore the possibili-
ties of motherhood in her rearrangement of the scheme of things.

A. B. Walkley in the *London Times* (October 17, 1895):

The author of *The Second Mrs. Tanqueray* and *The Notorious Mrs. Ebbsmith* still
seeks his inspiration among the more painful problems of social life. In the intensity and the harrowing character of its emotions *The Benefit of the Doubt*, which
was given last night at the Comedy Theatre, yields nothing to either of these
plays. Mr. Pinero is careful, it is true, at the close of an extremely long story
replete with character but almost destitute of incident, to suggest that there
may be a silver lining to the cloud which overhangs his *dramatis personae*, but
even that consolation is problematical. All that can safely be averred is that the
spectators' attention is absorbed by a distressing, yet curiously sympathetic
story, in which nothing of the perversity of human nature is extenuated, and
which ends on something like a note of interrogation. It is to the Divorce Court
that Mr. Pinero in this instance has gone for his dramatic material, or rather to a
situation which has been created by the machinery of the Divorce Court, before
the rising of the curtain, in the lives of two families. . . . .

Mrs. Allingham has brought suit against her husband for judicial separation
on the ground of his relations with Mrs. Fraser, and the suit has been dismissed,

Mrs. Fraser receiving "the benefit of the doubt," though severely lectured by the judge for her "indiscretion." Such is the starting point of the story, which thus becomes a minute and searching study of the human heart, and especially the female heart, under exceptionally trying conditions. What is Mrs. Fraser's first impulse upon emerging from the Divorce Court, innocent in deed and intention, but with the terrible millstone of the doubt hanging around her neck? It is to live down the scandal with her husband's help; and to him accordingly she makes an appeal in that sense with the concurrence of her family. But he is of a cold and reserved nature, and does not see matters in the same light. His pride as a gentleman has been deeply wounded at the dragging of his name through the mire of the Divorce Court. He is all for hiding his shame in a life of retirement abroad. Indeed, the marriage on general grounds has been a failure. . . . .

William Archer in the *World* (October 17, 1895):

Since he produced *The Second Mrs. Tanqueray* Mr. Pinero's position has been a peculiar one. He has drawn down on himself the wrath—yes, the contemptuous and vindictive wrath—of two classes of critics: those for whom the drama died with Congreve, and those for whom it only began to live with Ibsen. The former class hated the theatre simply *as* the theatre, and fiercely resented the suggestion that anything worth a moment's notice could come out of it. They felt it tactless on Mr. Pinero's part to exist at all, and they repaid the impertinence in kind.

The Notorious Mrs. Ebbsmith, despite its errors of detail, was a distinct advance on *The Second Mrs. Tanqueray*. It was larger in aim and subtler in method. It revealed, to my way of thinking (and I did not gloze the matter), a certain inadequacy in Mr. Pinero's philosophical equipment; but it showed nothing but progress in artistic power and sincerity. . . . .

A play, according to Alexander Dumas, should contain a painting, a judgment, and an ideal. Mr. Pinero has given us the painting; the judgment we need not insist upon, for judgments are generally wrong; but it would do no harm if, in subsequent works, he could manage to throw in a touch of the ideal.

It is, however, in the sphere of social comedy or drama that we are asked to recognize what Mr. Henry Arthur—must we stop there?—calls a "renascence." And it is here, beyond a doubt, that the advance is most palpable. We are more inclined to quarrel with the "re" of Mr. Arthur's term than with the "nascence"; for the present movement appears to us to differ from the above-mentioned pseudo-revivals in that it gives us a form of drama which we never had before. Robertsonian comedy was only the old comedy of manners in a new guise—the comedy of no-manners it was wittily called. It offered no criticism of life or of social institutions, beyond an assertion of the excellent but somewhat superficial maxim that fond hearts are more than coronets and simple faith than Norman blood. In the later works of Mr. Pinero, on the other hand, we have a drama of idea, in those of Mr. Henry Arthur—shall we say a melodrama of ideas? A stringent criticism of all social institutions is the chief feature in the intellectual life of the time; and in this criticism of the stage has begun to take an active and not incompetent part. All the tedious talk we have heard about "problem plays" and "sex plays" means nothing more than that the drama is at last beginning to seize upon and interpret the genuinely dramatic aspects of life. Yet it, too, died away, and we had to fall back upon imported *Diplomacies* and *Pink Dominoes*. Such experiences render us wary of hallooing before we are out of the wood, and incline us, even when a play deeply moves and interests us, to hedge our expressions of interest with a smile and a shrug. Moreover, the theatre, alone among the arts, tends to be estimated by a sort of average between its highest and its lowest productions. . . . .

A. B. Walkley in the *London Times* (April 10, 1899):

Intellectually Mr. Pinero stands alone among our dramatists, and he has written nothing cleverer than *The Gay Lord Quex*. But whether the roar of approval which greeted his appearance before the curtain on Saturday night may be taken as promising a popular success is doubtful. The mass of playgoers are sentimentalist, and this play entirely appeals to the head. There is not a tear— not even a moist eye—in any of its four acts. It is fresh, amusing, interesting; but it suggests bitter, not pleasant reflections. It is written for those who have outlived their illusions by a man who looks, clear-eyed, upon a world of which he has not much opinion. The school of critics which swears by the modern French play—not the old type of suggestive farce, but the work of serious writers like M. Lemaître and M. Lavendan—can hail Mr. Pinero as a convert to their view. *The Gay Lord Quex* in many ways suggests the French drama, and it was now and then difficult on Saturday evening—especially in the "bed-room scene"—not to imagine oneself in the Boulevards instead of the Strand. The lover of 48, the colourless *ingénue*, her young admirer who turns out to be altogether unworthy, the types of society who flit through the piece—they all seem to belong more to Paris than to London. If the piece moves the average theatregoer as it moved the first night audience, it will show that a change has come over the public taste.

Lord Quex is a type of the "man with a past" just as Mrs. Tanqueray was Mr. Pinero's idea of the "woman with a past." The woman finds her past tied around her neck like a millstone dragging her downwards all her life. The man (so Mr. Pinero will have it) can with a little trouble shake off his past like an old garment and scarcely retain even the memory of its burden. Mr. Pinero seems determined to show that "it's never too late to love." In *The Princess and the Butterfly* he insisted that a man of 40 was not past falling in love, in just the same impulsive fashion as a boy of 18. In *The Gay Lord Quex* the author goes a step further. Lord Quex is 48, with the reputation of having been very gay indeed.

But at 48 he falls in love with the "typical creamy English girl." He is so genuinely in love that for her sake he has become a reformed character. So he says at the beginning of the play. So we believe at the end, when he has fairly proved it. It is, in fact, the testing of Lord Quex's good resolutions that makes the play. There is a long list of characters, but the action of the piece is really left to no more than two—to Mr. Hare, who has never appeared to greater advantage than as this reformed rake of polished manners and shrewd ready wit, and to Miss Irene Vanbrugh, for whom Saturday evening was a veritable triumph. . . . . The scene (Quex goes to the Duchess' apartments merely to return her presents, and presently Sophy is discovered at the keyhole) which follows between Quex and the girl who is determined to ruin his chance with Miss Eden is indeed the most ingenious Mr. Pinero has ever written. The Duchess has been sent away by Quex to share a friend's room on pretence of "nerves." . . . .

It is a page torn from the book of life. The pity is that it should not be a page relating some less ignoble incident. Nothing can take from it its undeniable humanity and interest. But, when it is over, one could wish the playwright had had a finer theme for so supreme an effort than a combat of wits between a roué, who has to shuffle out of a discreditable past, and a young woman who, though it be for a good motive, has descended to immodesty and mean cunning.

The ending is natural, but unromantic. Indeed, there is no romance and very little sentiment in the play, and it must be confessed that, witty and brilliant and abounding in observation as it is, it shows us a world that is not attractive to contemplate. A world which spends its mornings in manicure shops and palmists' apartments—a world which keeps French novels that are "rather—you know—rather" in its bedroom and pretends to admire them for their "exquisitely polished style"; a world of midnight appointments in women's boudoirs—is not a pleasant or an edifying spectacle. The foolish and vulgar women of society, represented by Miss Fortesque and Miss Mona Oran, are tiresome and detestable, but they serve the satirist's purpose. . . . .

William Archer in the *World* (March 25, 1901):

Iris is scarcely to be regarded as an entertainment bidding for applause, but rather as an event happening in our midst, which imposes itself upon us as a thing fated, inevitable. We may or may not find it agreeable to contemplate, but it attracts our thoughts in spite of ourselves. Its place in theatrical, in literary history it is impossible to forecast; but that it will have a place, that it is a thing no historian of the intellectual movement of our time can afford to disregard, is already abundantly manifest. . . . .

In point of technical mastery, *Iris* is by a long way Mr. Pinero's finest achievement. The Ardale scene made a slight flaw in the otherwise admirably-woven texture of *The Second Mrs. Tanqueray;* and in each of the intermediate plays there have been marked inequalities of workmanship. *The Notorious Mrs. Ebbsmith* and *The Benefit of the Doubt* tailed off at the end. *The Princess and the Butterfly* wavered somewhat disconcertingly between the key of comedy and that of drama. In *Trelawny of the "Wells"* there were two strong and two comparatively weak acts: in *The Gay Lord Quex* (to my thinking) there was one superb act standing out from surroundings that were not only inferior but almost unworthy. You shall look in vain for such inequalities in *Iris*. From the first line to the last, everything is perfectly vitalized. There is not a superfluous word in the dialogue, and yet there is no sense of mechanical overcondensation—the dry, harsh, Euclid-like concision affected by one or two French playwrights of the day. . . . .

Is Iris Bellamy as well-observed as she is vividly projected?

Here I think there is a distinction to be drawn. Iris is wonderfully true so far as she goes, but she is a trifle incomplete. Mr. Pinero seems to me to have evaded, to have skipped, the crucial scene of his play—the scene of her installation in the Park Street flat.

A. B. Walkley in the *London Times* (September 23, 1901):

There is a sense—not strictly accurate, but permissible, perhaps, by "extension"—in which Mr. Pinero's new five-act drama, *Iris*,—together with *The Second Mrs. Tanqueray* and *The Notorious Mrs. Ebbsmith* and *The Benefit of the Doubt* might be said to form a tetralogy. These four plays are bound together not by any continuity of story, but by identity of theme. Each portrays an erring woman and her fate. The woman's fate is, of course, the denouement of the play; and it has always seemed to us hithertofore that in his denouements was to be found Mr. Pinero's weak point. They were apt to be arbitrary or to shirk logical results. Paula Tanqueray committed suicide, and sudden death is a cheap plot-solution; not so cheap, however, as the "whitewashing" of Agnes Ebbsmith and Theophila Fraser by the aid, spiritual or social, of the Anglican Church. In *Iris*, and in our judgment for the first time, Mr. Pinero does not shrink from the real denouement. And it must have cost him much to nerve himself to it. For the denouement of *Iris* overwhelms the spectator with horror. There is hardly room for pity. Indeed, there are no tears throughout the piece, save the *lacrymae rerum*. Further, although the denouement is felt to be exactly right, the spectator does not foresee it. At no step in the play does one foresee the next step, and yet, so soon as anything happened, one feels that it must have happened, and just in that way. This means, of course, what we knew already, that Mr. Pinero has at least one quality of the great dramatist, the art of stimulating curiosity, of stimulating it to a degree wherein it becomes almost gnawing anxiety, and then of satisfying it to the full. . . . . Paula was headstrong and perverse, Agnes steadily determined, Theophila rash. And this choice was all to Mr. Pinero's advantage, because will is the very stuff out of which drama is made. But here, in *Iris*, he has set himself a far harder task. For Iris Bellamy is will-less, or, what comes to the same thing, has a constantly divided will.

At the crisis of her fortunes, she has to choose, as she puts it herself, between recklessness and self-denial. But she has neither the courage for the one or the firmness for the other; her character is too weak. And in the penalty she pays for her weakness lies the tragedy of the play. She knows her own weakness of will, this rich young widow, and also her love of luxury. . . . . This first act has been most adroitly conducted. By a novel device of dropping the curtain for a few seconds at a time, so as to divide the evening into three "episodes," it has shown us Iris's nature and embarrassing situation between the two men, and the characters of those men. . . . .

Iris is a very powerful, very painful play, the most characteristic specimen of Mr. Pinero's art, a piece of literature and at the same time a piece of solid, living, throbbing drama.

A. B. Walkley in the *London Times* (February 2, 1906):

When Mr. Pinero is at his best we reckon ourselves as close upon the high water mark of theatrical enjoyment. In *His House in Order* he is at his very best. His master quality, by which we mean the quality specifically called dramatic is here seen at its maximum of energy. This or that playwright may show more "heart" than Mr. Pinero or a more delicate subtlety, a third may easily outclass him in intellectual gymnastic, but in his command of the resources of the stage for the legitimate purposes of the stage he is without a rival. The art of the drama is, quintessentially, the art of story-telling, as the sculptors say, "in the round." . . . .

Distaste for the obvious must not deter us from saying what will be said by everyone—that play ought to be called *The Second Mrs. Jesson*. That title, indeed, would be far more appropriate for the new play than *The Second Mrs. Tanqueray* for the old. We mean that in the earlier play the contrast between the first and second wife, though indicated was not worked out; whereas that contrast may be said to be the main motif of the new play. The character of the first Mrs. Tanqueray had no bearing on the fortunes of the second. . . . . He allows Hilary, the *raisonneur* of his play, to have an indignant explosion and to declare that the type, as a social pest, ought to be swept off the face of the earth. And this after Mr. Pinero had turned them to such handsome account, forcing them to contribute to public stock of harmless pleasure.

William Archer in the *World* (February 6, 1906):

On the right side of the impassable gulf which divides genius from talent, greatness from the most brilliant cleverness, there stands today a single English dramatist. Mr. Pinero, it is true, has not always done justice to himself or his art, and it is not long since his admirers were irritated by a deplorable misuse of

his great powers. All the more gratifying is it to recognize the splendid amends
he has made in a play which not only confirms him, by acclamation, in his place
of unchallenged supremacy, but marks, so far, his highest point of achievement.
In *His House in Order* Mr. Pinero has unquestionably achieved his master-work.
In power, in grasp, in vividness of emotional appeal, in easy strength of dialogue
and characterization no less than in faultless ingenuity of craftsmanship, this
play can safely challenge comparison with the finest of its predecessors from the
same hand. And as it excels them all in technical excellence, so also it surpasses
them in the tenderness and sincerity of its treatment of a singularly beautiful
theme, and in the scathing force of its satire upon one of the most noxious elements of English life. Here, at least, is a pre-eminently "well-made" play which
is also pre-eminently true, natural, and human—a play in which the hand of the
master-craftsman and the eye of the observant student of life and character have
worked in unison to produce such a genuine victory of art as comes all too rarely
in the history of the theatre.

APPENDIX III

BIBLIOGRAPHICAL NOTE

Thirty of Sir Arthur Pinero's plays were published by William Heinemann, Ltd., of London, in twenty-nine volumes; the list includes: *The Times, The Profligate, The Cabinet Minister, The Hobby-Horse, Lady Bountiful, The Magistrate, Dandy Dick, Sweet Lavender, The Schoolmistress, The Weaker Sex, The Amazons, The Second Mrs. Tanqueray, The Notorious Mrs. Ebbsmith, The Benefit of the Doubt, The Princess and the Butterfly, Trelawny of the "Wells," The Gay Lord Quex, Iris, Letty, A Wife without a Smile, His House in Order, The Thunderbolt, Mid-Channel, The "Mind the Paint" Girl, Preserving Mr. Panmure, The Big Drum, The Enchanted Cottage, The Freaks,* and *Two Plays* ("Dr. Harmer's Holidays" and "Child Man").

Inasmuch as publication was zealously guarded until the passage of the International Copyright Act of 1891, the list begins with Pinero's play of that year, *The Times.* For the first eleven volumes in this series (1891–95) Malcolm C. Salaman wrote interesting introductions. For *Two Plays,* Pinero himself wrote a "Foreword."

The "first editions" were, however, not for circulation; they were privately printed, and at the top of the paper cover appears this notice: "Printed—as Manuscript—*for Private Circulation only,*" or "Printed for use in the theatre, not for circulation."

In 1917 Clayton Hamilton edited *The Social Plays of Sir Arthur Wing Pinero* (4 vols.; New York: Dutton), with a brilliantly written general introduction and critical preface to each play. The plays included are *The Second Mrs. Tanqueray, The Notorious Mrs. Ebbsmith, The Benefit of the Doubt, Trelawny of the "Wells," The Gay Lord Quex, Iris, Letty, His House in Order, The Thunderbolt,* and *Mid-Channel.*

Sir Arthur Pinero has expressed his own ideas about playwriting in the following articles: "Preface" to Courtney's *Idea of Tragedy,* 1900; "Robert Louis Stevenson: The Dramatist," *Critic,* XLII (1900), 341 ff.; "Robert Browning as a Dramatist," *Transactions of the Royal Society of Literature,* XXXI (1912), 7 ff.; "The Theatre in the Seventies" in *The Eighteen-seventies* (Cambridge, 1929); and in the Foreword to *Two Plays* (London, 1930).

Hamilton Fyfe has written two books about Pinero: *Arthur Wing Pinero, Playwright* (London, 1902), and *Sir Arthur Pinero's Plays and Players* (London, 1930). The first book contains in its closing pages a list of Pinero's early plays and their casts, including material about some revivals, through the year 1901. The second book is a reorganization of the first, with much additional comment.

The most appreciative comment on Pinero's contribution to the drama is to be found in Archer's *The Drama Old and New* (Boston, 1923).

Paul Hamelius wrote *Arthur Wing Pinero und das Drama der Jetztzeit* (Brussels, 1900); it is of slight value. Wilibald Stöcker's short thesis, *Pinero's Dramen: Studien über Motive, Charaktere, und Technik* (Halle, 1911), is disappointing and of no value at all.

Among the articles there are three of popular rather than critical interest: J. P. Collin's, "The Plays of Sir Arthur Pinero" in the *Quarterly Review* (April, 1930); Edgar Holt's, "A Dramatic Jubilee—Arthur Pinero" in the *Fortnightly Review* (March, 1928); and Daniel Frohman's personal impressions in an early issue of the *Saturday Evening Post* (Philadelphia, 1910).

Of the dramatic critics of the day, two stand out: William Archer and A. B. Walkley. Walkley's *Drama and Life* (London, 1908), and *Playhouse Impressions* (London, 1912); and of Archer's many books, *English Dramatists of To-day* (London, 1882), *Study and Stage* (London, 1899), and *The Old Drama and the New* (New York, 1923), should in particular not be overlooked. William Archer's articles in the *World* and the *Fortnightly Review* are very important.

In England the *Theatre*, the *Stage*, the *Era*, the *Critic*, the *Saturday Review*, the *Athenaeum*, the *Fortnightly Review*, the *World*, the *Academy*, the *Quarterly Review*, the *Morning Post*, the *Telegraph*, the *Evening News*, and the *Standard* repay the hours spent with the *Index* to the *Times* as guide, searching for material about Pinero and the reception of his plays.

To list the books in which references to Pinero occur is to include the books about the theaters, the actors, the drama, and the playwrights from 1880 to the present time. The books in the following list contain material of particular interest: Agate's *At Half-Past Eight* (New York, 1923); Armstrong's *Shakespeare to Shaw* (London, 1913); the Bancrofts' *Recollections of Sixty Years* (London, 1909); Borsa's *The English Stage of Today* (London, 1908); Cunliffe's *Modern English Playwrights* (New York, 1927); Chandler's *Aspects of Modern Drama* (New York, 1914); Dickinson's *The Contemporary Drama of England* (Boston, 1922); Dukes's *Modern Dramatists* (Chicago, 1912); Filon's *The English Stage* (London, 1897); Hale's *Dramatists of To-day* (New York, 1911); Hamilton's *Conversations on Contemporary Drama* (New York, 1925); Howe's *Dramatic Portraits* (New York, 1913); Jameson's *The Modern Drama in Europe* (New York, 1920); and Nicoll's *British Drama: An Historical Survey* (New York, 1925).

During the writing of this book appeared A. E. W. Mason's *Sir George Alexander and the St. James's Theatre* (London, 1935) and F. S. Boas' *From Richardson to Pinero* (London, 1936). The former alludes sympathetically to Pinero; the latter praises Pinero as a writer about the theater as he found it but follows the errors in Hamilton Fyfe's two books.

INDEX TO PERSONS, PLAYS
AND THEATERS

139

DATE DUE